Psychological Skills Training. Application to Elite Sport Performance

Elite Sport Performance

ISBN 0-9817180-8-6

Boris Blumenstein, Ph.D.

The Wingate Institute, Israel

Yitzhak Weinstein, Ph.D.

Ohalo Academic College

Tel-Hai Academic College, Israel

Contents

Preface

The main goal of this book is to integrate psychological skills training (PST) with other training processes of the athletic preparation program; several means of achieving this goal in numerous sport types are described. Additionally, we wish to create a relevant body of knowledge for sport psychologists, coaches, athletes, physical education students, and scientists. We trust that the information presented herein will help to improve training processes and to upgrade the preparation of athletes for competition.

The chapters contain numerous real-life examples and practical tips of applied sport psychology with top elite athletes and European, World, and Olympic medalists from different sports. Both authors have worked with elite athletes; the first author focused mainly on scientific and psychological services to elite athletes, while the second author was mainly involved with the scientific (e.g. physiological and psycho-physiological) services to elite athletes. Linking theory and practice can affect athletic performance and achievements in competition. While many textbooks and scientific papers have discussed aspects of individual and team sports and provide information on psychological aspects of sport activity, this book focuses on PST and its application to the athletic preparation process. The book provides coaches, athletes, and sport psychologists with theoretical (Chapters 1, 2) and practical (Chapters 3, 4) guidance. In addition to presenting major theoretical concepts related to psychological preparation in sport, this book also shares the vast experience of a sport psychology consultant who has worked with top-level athletes, clubs, and national and Olympic teams for over 35 years.

Chapter 1 provides a short overview of the critical phases within an annual training program and various preparations in each phase. Psychological preparation is discussed in terms of its role as an integral part of the training programs; the chapter contains numerous examples illustrating the application of this preparation to enhance athletic performance. Chapter 2 focuses on peak performance and psychological skills, with examples in various sport types. Additionally, the association between mental training techniques and psychological skills is described. The chapter combines research findings of PST with practical applications. Chapter 3 provides information about the applications of psychological skills programs for performance enhancement, as well as the implications of PST to the training process for individual and team sports. The authors conclude the chapter with common issues they have addressed when working with elite athletes. Chapter 4 discusses the role and place of the sport psychology consultant in the training process, including cooperation with the coach, medical, scientific and professional staff. Special attention is given to ethical issues. Chapter 5 provides information on where and how to begin PST, and evaluates PST and its limitations. Finally, this chapter attempts to predict the future of PST.

We wish to thank Ms. Dinah Olswang from the Zinman College at the Wingate Institute, who has been part of our professional team for the language editing of this book. Thanks are also due to the publisher, Mr. Yosef Johnson, for his valuable advice, encouragement and support during each phase of the preparation of this project, and to Professors Gershon Tennebaum, Michael Bar-Eli, and Ronnie Lidor for their many years of inspiration. We would also like to express our appreciation to the scientific project "Kamea" for its support. Special thanks are due to the athletes and the coaches, without whom this book could not be a reality. Finally, special thanks to our spouses, Tali B. and Ayelet W. for their continuous support, love and thoughtful encouragement.

Chapter 1. Psychological Preparation is an Integral Part of Athletic High Performance

This chapter contains a brief overview of the main phases within an annual training program, as well as various preparations in each phase. Psychological skills training (PST) is discussed in terms of its role as an integral part of the sport training program.

<u>About sport training.</u>

Sport training is an essential component of the athletic preparation system, representing a unique pedagogical process based on the utilization of numerous physical exercises. The main object of athletic training is to develop the various athletic qualities and skills required for peak performance in modern sport.

Experts in the theory and methodology of sport training maintain that athletic preparation is composed of physical, technical, tactical, and psychological preparations (e.g., Bompa, 1999; Carrera & Bompa, 2007; Harre, 1982; Platonov, 1986). Each of these preparations is mutually linked and interrelated, and influence and define each other (Balague, 2000; Blumenstein, Lidor, & Tenenbaum, 2005, 2007; Dosil, 2006). For example, in considering technical preparation, one should appreciate that this preparation is based and depends on physical preparation and on the developmental level of various characteristics of physical fitness, such as endurance, strength, power, speed, and flexibility.

However, the level of various motor skills (e.g., endurance) is linked to psychological stability, technical economy, and special tactical plans during competition stress. Tactical preparation is linked to technical, physical, and psychological preparations. Naturally, psychological preparation is an integral component of all preparation stages, and its elements strengthen other preparation components (Blumenstein, Lidor, & Tenenbaum, 2007). Each training session and practice includes a psychological ingredient or component. This holds true for all active coaches and athletes; indeed, psychological factors are an integral part of each practice session and on every training day. Details of the four preparation components, including their major goals, are illustrated in Figure 1.1.

Figure 1.1. Training processes used for athletic preparation, and their main goals and elements

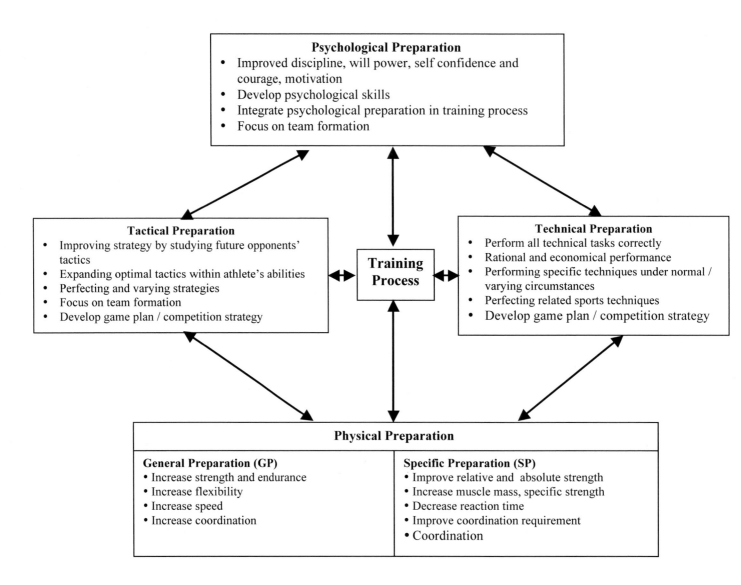

The foremost goal of the physical preparation is to develop the relevant physical fitness components (e.g., endurance, strength, flexibility, speed) required for the specific performance in a particular sport event; that is, to refine the specific motor abilities required to attain a high level of achievement throughout the competition phase (Carrera & Bompa, 2007; Harre, 1982). During the physical preparation athletes must carry out difficult and monotonous work, with an endless number of repetitions. Of course, the physical preparation is very specific for the type of sport in which the athlete is engaged, and demands a high level of motivation, self-discipline, consistency, and stability. The relationship between physical and psychological preparation and psychological factors of excellence has received much attention in the literature over the years (e.g., Abbott, Button, Pepping, & Collins, 2005; Collins & MacPherson, 2007; Orlick & Partington, 1988).

The goal of technical preparation is to enable the athlete to effectively acquire the skills needed for optimal performance during competition (Bompa, 1999). Technical preparation is linked and correlated with physical, tactical, and psychological preparations (Schack & Bar-Eli, 2007). For example, in times when a soccer player experiences difficulties in his physical preparation, he may demonstrate his brilliant technique on one or two occasions but will not be capable of performing well throughout an entire 90-minute match. Soccer players usually spend more time in defense than in offense, and are expected to function well in every match. However, due to poor cardiovascular (CV) fitness, players may fatigue prematurely (Mohr, Krustrup & Bangsbo, 2005). Psychological intervention may help in such instances in which poor CV fitness limits performance. It should be noted that a player who is well prepared technically but with poor physical preparation might not be able to execute tactical schemes in real time situations (Mohr et al., 2005).

The main goal of tactical preparation is to provide athletes with the strategic knowledge required to effectively execute the skills they have acquired and perfected in real competition (Henschen, Statler, & Lidor, 2007). Athletes with good tactical preparation are capable of correctly planning,

3

taking into account the opponents' maneuvers and coping with rapidly changing conditions. Good tactical preparation is expected to be linked to other phases of preparation (Bomba, 1999; Henschen, Statler, & Lidor, 2007). An athlete with good tactical preparation is less likely to be limited (i.e., unable to accomplish the tactical plan) by poor physical preparation. Athletes with poor technical preparation usually make many technical errors and cannot fully realize their tactical plan. Additionally, poor psychological preparation prevents athletes from concentrating during competitions, and on some occasions may trigger them to forfeit a fight or a match even before it starts.

High levels of performance and achievement are the result of many years of well planned, precise, methodical hard training. During this period, the athletes adapt their physiological functions to suit the specific requirements of the sport event. Carrera and Bompa (2007) argued that the greater the degree of adaptation, the better the athletic performance.

Competition is the main regulatory control of peak athletic performance, and thus it is an inseparable ingredient of the modern training process; present elite sport is typified by a very high level of competition. During the last three summer (2000, 2004, 2008) and winter (2002, 2006, 2010) Olympic Games, there was a 1.5- to 2-fold rise in the number of countries competing for a given number of medals. For example, in addition to the country's traditional sports, China was successful in volleyball, track and field, swimming, rhythmic gymnastics; Kenya and Ethiopia – long distance running; Italy – skiing, rhythmic gymnastics; the USA – artistic and rhythmic gymnastics, figure skating. Furthermore, prior to the fall of the Soviet Union, the USSR competed for a given medal as one country. Today 15 independent countries, which were formerly part of one USSR team, compete for the same medal (e.g., Ukraine, Georgia, Russia, and Lithuania – wrestling, judo, weightlifting; Azerbaijan, Russia, Ukraine, Belarus – rhythmic gymnastics, track and field; Belarus, Russia, Ukraine – shooting, track and field, rowing).

The past decade was characterized by an improved system of sport training: increase total volume of training workloads; number and level of competitions; balance between training loads and competitions; training loads and recovery; proper nutrition and rest. There is a strong relationship between training and the specific needs of a sport, thus the duration of general preparation is reduced, but specific preparation is increased, and part of it is carried out during periods between seasons (Issurin, 2007; Platonov, 1986;). This approach allows most elite athletes to maintain a high level of physical fitness during these in-between periods. In modern training programs the role of specific preparation is rising, and with the advanced science and technology easily available today there is a growing use of non-traditional means of athlete preparation, such as special and high-technology equipment, high altitude training methods (e.g., live high-train low, live low-train high), tight physiological control by means of periodic laboratory and field tests, use of nutritional supplementation, etc.

Training program for elite sport.

Training may be viewed as a systematic and continuous athletic activity that is progressively growing. The main objective of training is to increase the athlete's work capacity and skill capabilities, and to develop strong psychological qualities (Carrera & Bompa, 2007). A typical training program for elite athletes is composed of three main phases: preparation, competition, and transition. The competition is considered as the central phase, during which the athlete is required to attain the highest performance level, to achieve the best results, or to be at the top place. The preparation and the transition phases of the training program are essential in enabling the athlete to attain top performance (Bompa, 1999).

Each of the training phases has unique characteristics and objectives. For example, in the preparation phase, the athlete develops a general framework of the physical, technical, tactical, and psychological preparations for the upcoming competition phase (Blumenstein, Lidor, & Tenenbaum,

2007; Bompa, 1999). The preparation phase concludes with general and specific preparation programs (GP and SP, respectively). The main goal of GP is to improve general athletic and physical abilities, while the main goal for SP is to enhance the abilities and skills required for a specific sport type.

During the competition phase the athlete attempts to achieve his/her best results in as many competitions as possible. One cannot escape noticing the rise in the number of competitions and the substantial increase in the financial motivation of top athletes in modern sport. For example, a series of Grand Prix or Golden League, Diamond league world and continental cups is associated with significant 6-figure financial rewards. During a training year, elite cycle-sprinters may participate in as many as 200-250 starts, and in separate months they may start more than 40 times. Elite swimmers can participate in 25-30 competitions with 100-120 starts, etc. (Issurin, 2007; Platonov, 1986).

The transition phase enables the athlete to take part in physical and psychological rest and relaxation. However, elite athletes are advised to remain active during this phase, to be better prepared for the next preparation phase.

In Olympic, World, and European finals, the best elite athletes compete with equivalent physical, technical, and tactical preparations, but in these stressful situations special psychological skills can play a key role in their success. According to Williams and Krane (2001), most athletes and coaches acknowledge that 40%-90% of their success in sport may be attributed to mental factors. Moreover, surveys of elite athletes from various countries revealed that about 80% of the athletes rated psychological preparation as being very important in their professional athletic success (Heishman & Bunker, 1989; Raalte & Petitpas, 2009).

<u>Psychological preparation is an integral part of the training program</u>

The goal of the psychological preparation is to provide athletes with task-specific psychological techniques, which allow them to overcome emotional and mental barriers such as fear of failure, high anxiety, loss of "attentional-focusing", and low self-confidence (Anshel, 2005; Blumenstein, Lidor, & Tenenbaum, 2007; Vealey, 2007).

Presently, psychological preparation is an integral part of training programs in both individual and team sports (Blumenstein, Lidor, & Tenenbaum, 2005; Henschen, 2001; Lidor, Blumenstein, & Tenenbaum, 2007; Serpa & Rodrigues, 2001; Vernacchia, 2003). However, one should carefully consider the current phase of the training program in which athletes are involved and apply more specific psychological strategies (or their combinations) accordingly. In other words, the relationship between psychological preparation and the training program should be strengthened. Indeed, in one of his training theories Platonov (1986) described a balance between GP, SP, and technical preparation in the training process of elite track and field athletes (see Table 1.1).

Table 1.1. Distribution of percent time given to each of the three training program phases: general preparation (GP), specific preparation (SP) and technical preparation (TP) in track and field (modified from Platonov, 1986, p. 219)

Track and Field Event	Preparation Phase			Competition Phase			Transition Phase		
	GP	SP	TP	GP	SP	TP	GP	SP	TP
Sprint, Jumps	30	50	20	20	50	30	80	10	10
Long distance run	15	80	5	5	90	5	45	50	5
Throwers	30	30	40	20	30	50	80	10	10

Table 1.1 illustrates the importance of applying specific preparation close to major sport events. The incidence of major events (competitions) has been increased in modern sport training. GP is mainly applied in the transition phase. The sport psychologist consultant is expected to recognize the importance of this balance in order to stay current in the training process, and to understand which psychological programs (packages) should be applied during a given period.

The impact of the evolving perspectives of the training process on PST programs is detailed in Table 1.2, which also describes recommended psychological techniques and their objectives during the three preparation phases.

Table 1.2. Recommended psychological techniques, including examples, and their objectives during three phases of the preparation program. Where ↑ improved/increased.

Phase	Psychological technique	Objectives	Application and duration
General Preparation (GP)	Relaxation	Mental recovery	20-25 min – end of the week 10-15 min, 1-2 times/wk 5-10 min, 3-4 times/wk
	Imagery (nature pictures)	Mental recovery	10-15 min, 1-2 times/wk
	Music (relaxation oriented)	Mental recovery	15-20 & 5-10 min, 1-2 times/wk
	Biofeedback (training & games)	Mental recovery	10-15 min, 1-2 times/wk
	Goal setting	Self-confidence, ↑motivation	10-15 min, 1time/wk 5 min, 1-2 times/wk
	Combinations: Relaxation & imagery Relaxation & music Relaxation & biofeedback	Mental recovery	20-25 min at laboratory settings, 1-2 times/wk
Special Preparation (SP)	Relaxation	Focusing attention & arousal regulation	1-5 min @ training settings 5-10 sec @ practice between exercises, fights, games
	Imagery	Mental readiness, focusing on aspects of technical-tactical performance	1-3 min @ practice; warm-up, between exercises, fights, games
	Self-talking	Mental readiness, self confidence	10-15 sec @ before exercises, fights, games, @ warm-ups
	Concentration exercises	Preparation for performance; mental readiness	5-10 min @ lab settings
	Breathing exercises	Mental readiness Mental recovery	1-2 min @ training; before and after performance
	Biofeedback training	Mental readiness, self confidence	10-30 sec @ laboratory settings. 1-2 times/wk
	Reaction training program	Mental readiness, ↑psycho-motor skills	10-15 min @ lab settings 1-2 times/wk
Competition	Relaxation & music; Relaxation & imagery	Mental readiness Mental recovery	5-10 min; weekend or during competition settings, between exercises, fights, practices
	Imagery	Mental readiness, focusing on aspects of technical-tactical performance	1.30 min – rhythmic gymnastics 5 min – judo Swim race – swimming distance w/time Basketball – combinations Rowing, kayak – race distance
	Self-talking	Mental readiness, focusing on aspects of technical-tactical	10-15 sec @ competition and training settings, before performance or analysis of earlier competitions

			performance
	Breathing exercise	Arousal regulation	10-15 sec @ competition and training settings, before performance
	Pre-competition mental readiness	Mental readiness	@competition settings; before performance
	Biofeedback training	↑Concentration and self confidence	5-10 min @ lab settings: 1-2 times/wk
	Reaction training program	↑ Psycho-motor skills	10-15 min @ lab settings: 1-2 times/wk
Transition	Relaxation	Mental recovery	10-15 min; 1 time/wk @ lab settings or @ home
	Music	Mental recovery	10-15 min; 1 time/wk @ lab settings
	Biofeedback games	Mental recovery; self confidence	10-15 min; 1 time/wk @ lab settings

In the preparation phase the athlete trains with: a large number of low-intensity exercises and repetitions, monotonous loads, a difficult daily regime, a high volume of training with firm coach demands, etc. Psychological techniques are applied in this period to provide the athlete with mental recovery techniques, increased sport motivation, and strengthened stability and confidence. These consist of relaxation (20-25 min), special music sessions (15-20 min or shorter duration); imagery featuring nature pictures; video clips (10-15 min); biofeedback training with different games (10-15 min); and combinations of these techniques, such as relaxation and imagery, relaxation and music, and relaxation and biofeedback. The effectiveness of using each of these techniques in mental training is described in the literature (e.g., Blumenstein, Bar-Eli, &Tennenbaum, 2002; Dosil, 2006; Statler & Henschen, 2009; Vealey, 2007; Williams, 2001).

As noted above, in the preparation phase key SP and technical preparations are increased, and the psychological preparation consists of concentration exercises, imagery with focusing on technical-tactical aspects of performance, short relaxation exercises of 1,3,5, min during training settings, etc. Moreover, some of these strategies are supplemented with numerous distractions, such as negative-positive motivation instructions, recorded competitive sounds, demands and norms, punishments, etc. (see Chapter III for more details).

During the competition phase (at the end of the preparation phase) the athletes are presented with real environmental factors which are related to actual competition or game situations. Here, the psychological techniques practice duration should be almost identical to the duration of the actual competition. For example, a judo fight lasts 5 min, thus the imagery duration should also be 5 min; likewise, the duration of an exercise in rhythmic gymnastics lasts 90 sec, therefore the imagery technique should also last 90 sec, etc.

It is of great importance for us to present several examples detailing numerous types of psychological preparation integration with other preparations, during annual as well as weekly training programs. We have chosen fencing and team rhythmic gymnastics as representative sport events to describe the periodization and planning processes of psychological preparation during the different phases of the training program. These examples (cases) took place in real life situations and were carried out during the training programs of elite athletes in recent years.

Case 1: Fencing

This sport places great importance on technical and tactical preparation, well-founded physical preparation, and very comprehensive psychological preparation process. Accordingly, Howard's (2006) technical preparation approach included numerous exercises for improving footwork and blade work, as well as fundamental fencing actions: attack, parry, riposte, parry, counter riposte, counterattack, and counter time. Since fencing is a tactical sport, its tactics are the proper and precise application of fencing techniques in order to score touches and not be scored against. Fencing motions must develop into instantaneous reflexes rather than ones which require the fencer's assessment prior to the execution of each motion. Additionally, each motion must be executed in the most economical manner possible. That is, it must be executed at the correct distance, with the correct timing, and with no wasted energy on unnecessary motions. In addition, a fencer learns not only to accurately assess his/her opponent but also the opponent's individual movement-responses (Howard, 2006). Good, tactically-prepared fencers control the attack by making the opponent respond by attacking or defending at inopportune times, in addition to using as little energy as possible by setting up situations that cause the opponent to act or react and by so doing, exhausting their energy reserves.

The mental preparation of fencers includes the developing of reasoning (interpretation) skills, such as concentration, self-control, relaxation, and self-talking. Fencers usually function under dynamic situations which demand various uses of cognitive processes, such as anticipating movements made by the opponent, making decisions, executing the planned act, etc.

In summary, the fencer is expected to be able to respond swiftly with high levels of attention, consistency, and stability. Table 1.3 illustrates the annual training program of an elite 21 year old female fencer who competed in the 2008 Olympic Games in Beijing.

Table 1.3. Annual preparation plan for a female fencer during the 2006-2007 season

Periodization Month	Preparation				Competition Calendar
	Physical	**Technical**	**Tactical**	**Psycho-logical**	
Preparation Phase (GP)					
October, 2006	++++	+	++	++	
November, 2006	++++	+++	++	++	
(SP)					
December, 2006	++	++++	+++	+++	
January, 2007	++	++++	++++	++++	+
Competition Phase					
February, 2007	++	+++	+++	++	
March, 2007	+	+	+	+	+++
April, 2007	++	++	+++	++	+
May, 2007	+++	+++	++++	++++	
June, 2007	++	+++	++++	+++	+
July, 2007	+	+++	+++	++	• E
August, 2007	+	++	+++	+	• U
September, 2007	+	+++	++++	++	
October, 2007		++	+++	++	• W
Transition Phase					
November, 2007	++			+	

Where:
+ weekly phase
GP general preparation
SP specific preparation
+ tournament Grand Prix
• European (**E**), World Championships (**W**), and Universiada (**U**).

The main objective of this program was to enable fencers to perform at peak ability during major fencing events such as European and World Championships, and Universiada. Among the psychological techniques applied during the preparation phase (October-January, 2007) were relaxation, imagery, self-talk, biofeedback training, and a special reaction-time program. All mental training sessions were implemented in three settings: laboratory, training, and home assignments given to the fencer to do in her free time. Each session lasts 50-60 min, once a week.

During the competition phase (January-October, 2007) the fencer was exposed to a variety of actual environmental factors related to combat situations, such as competitive noises and competition fragments (match) with simulations using video clips, positive and negative verbal comments (e.g., "You are doing great"; "Fantastic"; "It's not your day"; "You can do better than that"). The simulations were combined with applications of psychological techniques such as imagery (e.g., imaging successful performances), attention-focusing on relevant cues (before and during the fights), and self-talk (before, during, and after the matches).

In the transition phase the fencer was instructed to maintain a low level of physical activity. Psychological recovery techniques were implemented, such as relaxation, music, breathing exercises, and biofeedback games (Blumenstein, Lidor, & Tenenbaum, 2007).

Following is a typical protocol of the one mental session undertaken by a female fencer during the preparation phase (see Table 1.4).

Table 1.4. Example of one psychological training session of a female fencer during the **preparation** phase. Where GSR=galvanic skin response, EMG=electromyogram, BFB=Bio-Feedback

Place: Sport Psychology Lab **Day**: Monday, November, 2006 **Time**: 09:00-10:00	
Introductory part	Developing motivation and positive thinking
Main part	Attention-focusing exercises, 20 sec X 3-4 times with • GSR BFB (good results: Δ 30-40KΩ during 20 sec). • Reaction Training program (RTP) – 15 (simple) – 30 (choice) – 30 (discrimination) reaction X 3 times (goal to achieve in simple about 165-170 μsec; in choice – 175-180 μsec; in discrimination: 165-170 μsec) with balance in each exercise between "fast" (reaction response < 200 μsec) and "slow" reaction responses (> 200 μsec) 7/3 or 8/2. More details about this program are described in Chapter 3 and in Blumenstein, Lidor, and Tenenbaum (2007). • Imagery which focuses on a fight against an opponents from Europe with dominant tactical side of match.
Final part	Muscle relaxation with EMG BFB accompanied by special relaxation music, 5-7 min.
Remarks	Completed all of the training sessions assignments

During the competition phase we provided mental sessions with different difficulties; see Chapter III. Following are typical protocols of the mental session undertaken by a female fencer during the competition phase (see Table 1.5).

Table 1.5. Example of one psychological training session of a female fencer during the **competition** phase.

Place: Sport Psychology Lab Day: Monday, January, 2007 Time: 13:00-14:00	
Introductory part	Analyzing the past week and developing motivation and goal setting according to the current training situations
Main part	• Attention-focusing exercises with GSR BFB: 10 sec X 3-4 times. • Relaxation-excitation exercises "waves" with EMG/GSR BFB with VCR impact (i.e., competition noises and fragments): 20 sec X 2-3 times • Imagery which focuses on a fight against possible opponents from Europe, special attention to relaxing non-dominant hand. All imagery process incorporated with competition voices. •
Final part	Muscle relaxation with EMG/GSR BFB 5-10 min.
Remarks	Special attention to relaxation of non-dominant hand

Case 2: Team rhythmic gymnastics

In this case the weekly training plan in the competition phase will be discussed. The rhythmic gymnastics team (five persons) practiced two times each day. In the morning at 08:00 they underwent a choreographic session (1.5 hours), and from 09:30 until 12:30 they performed rhythmic gymnastics elements and exercises on a carpet. The second training took place from 16:00 until 19:30-20:00, with the aim of improving rhythmic gymnastics combinations (e.g., with a ball, clubs, ribbons).

Psychological support in this period accompanied the trainings, and helped athletes to cope with stress. Individual and team mental sessions were provided, according to training situations and the personal demands of the athletes. Table 1.6 exemplifies a typical individual training session during the competition period.

Table 1.6. Example of individual psychological training session of rhythmic gymnast during the **competition** phase.

Place: Sport Psychology Lab **Day**: Tuesday, May 2007 **Time**: 13:30-14:15	
Introductory part	Concentration exercises – 3 X 20 sec with GSR BFB
Main part	Imagery 2 exercises, X3 times each, e.g., ball and ribbon, with time control Relaxation with music – 15 min
Final part	BFB games – 5 min.
Remarks	Special attention to emotional expression

We met each day with the gymnasts during practice (morning-evening training) or during individual-team mental sessions. A total of 3-4 weekly mental meetings were provided during this competition phase, especially prior to important competitions (see Chapter 3 for more details).

These examples have been presented to strengthen our argument for the need of a strong relationship between psychological preparation and the other types of preparations. A mental training consultant is expected to understand the role and place of each of these preparations in the training program, and should be able to "readily and creatively integrate mental and physical training into an integrative process" (Vealey, 2007, p. 292).

Conclusions

1. Contemporary sport is characterized by high-level competition, and in the future athletes will most likely compete at even higher levels. This will have an effect on modern and future sport training approaches, which should constantly be altered to accommodate the rising demands. For example, presently there is a strong correlation between physical training systems carried out from childhood until those at the peak of a career as an adult. Similarly, mental preparation should follow the same reasoning, and be carried out together with physical training from childhood until the peak adult career, in a well-coordinated manner based on sound methodological and scientific foundations.

2. Modern athletic training processes are typified by worthy tendencies, such as increased competition practice and number of competitions and the longer duration of the competition period. These tendencies call for a rethinking of the traditional training approach. The annual season should be restructured to allow for the dynamic and rapidly changing and growing demands placed on elite athletes.

3. We believe that given the time and level of physical training limits to human abilities, the magnitude of psychological and mental training programs will be increased and will occupy larger segments of the total preparation of elite athletes.

4. The psychological consultant is expected to have a broad and comprehensive understanding of modern sport and its demands during the preparation process of elite athletes for peak performance during competitions.

References

Abbot, A., Button, C. Pepping, G., & Collins, D. (2005). Unnatural selection: Talent identification and development in sport. *Nonlinear Dynamics, Psychology, and Life Sciences, 1,* 61-88.

Anshel, M. (2005). Strategies for preventing and managing stress and anxiety in sport. In D. Hackfort, J. Duda, & R. Lidor (Eds.), *Handbook on research in applied sport and exercise psychology: International perspectives* (pp. 199-215). Morgantown, WV: Fitness Information Technology.

Balague, G. (2000). Periodization of psychological skills training. *Journal of Science and Medicine in Sport,* 3, 1230-1237.

Blumenstein, B., Bar-Eli, M., & Tenenbaum, G. (Eds.) (2002), *Brain and body in sport and exercise: Biofeedback applications in performance enhancement.* Chichester, West Sussex: Wiley.

Blumenstein, B., Lidor, R., & Tenenbaum, G. (2005). Periodization and planning of psychological preparation in elite combat sport programs: The case of judo. *International Journal of Sport and Exercise Psychology, 3,* 7-25.

Blumenstein, B., Lidor, R., & Tenenbaum, G. (2007). Sport Psychology and the theory of sport training: An integrated approach. In Blumenstein, B., Lidor, R., & Tenenbaum, G *(Eds.). Psychology of sport training* (pp. 8-18). Oxford: Meyer & Meyer Sport.

Bompa, T. (1999). *Periodization: The theory and methodology of training* (4th ed.). Champaign, IL: Human Kinetics.

Carrera, M., & Bompa, T. (2007). Theory and methodology of training: General perspective. In B. Blumenstein, R. Lidor, & G. Tenenbaum (Eds.), *Psychology of sport training* (pp. 19-39). Oxford: Meyer & Meyer Sport.

Collins, D., & MacPherson, A. (2007). Psychological factors of physical preparation. In B. Blumenstein, R. Lidor, & G. Tenenbaum (Eds.), *Psychology of sport training* (pp. 40-61). Oxford: Meyer & Meyer Sport.

Dosil, J. (Ed.). (2006). *The sport psychologist's handbook: A guide for sport-specific performance enhancement.* Chichester, West Sussex: Wiley.

Harre, D. (Ed.). (1982). *Principles of sport training: Introduction to theory and methods of training.* Berlin: Sport Verlag.

Heishman, M. & Bunker, L. (1989). Use of mental preparation strategies by international elite female lacrosse players from five countries. *The Sport Psychologist, 3,* 14-22.

Henschen, K. (2001). Lessons from sport psychology consulting. In G. Tenenbaum (Ed.), *The practice of sport psychology* (pp. 77-88). Morgantown, WV: Fitness Information Technology.

Henschen, K., Statler, T., & Lidor, R. (2007). Psychological factors of tactical preparation. In B. Blumenstein, R. Lidor, & G. Tenenbaum (Eds.), *Psychology of sport training* (pp. 104-114). Oxford: Meyer & Meyer Sport.

Howard, R. (2006). Essentials of fencing technique. http://www.acfencers.com/essentials.html

Issurin, V. (2007). A modern approach to high-performance training: The block composition concept. In B. Blumenstein, R. Lidor, & G. Tenenbaum (Eds.), *Psychology of sport training* (pp. 216-235). Oxford: Meyer & Meyer Sport.

Lidor, R., Blumenstein, B., & Tenenbaum, G. (2007). Periodization and planning of psychological preparation in individual and team sports. In B. Blumenstein, R. Lidor, & G. Tenenbaum (Eds.), *Psychology of sport training* (pp. 137-161). Oxford: Meyer & Meyer Sport.

Mohr, M., Krustrup, P., & Bangsbo, J. (2005). Fatigue in soccer: A brief review. *Journal of Sports Sciences, 23,* 593-599

Orlick, T., & Partington, J. (1988). Mental links to excellence. *The Sports Psychologist, 2,* 105-130.

Platonov, V. N. (1986*). Preparation of the elite athlete.* Moscow: Physical Culture and Sport.

Raalte, J., & Petitpas, A. (2009). Sport psychology service provision at elite international competitions. In T. Hung, R. Lidor, & D. Hackfort (Eds.), *Psychology of Sport Excellence* (pp. 45-52). Mogantown, WV: Fitness Information Technology.

Schack, T., & Bar-Eli, M. (2007). Psychological factors of technical preparation. In B. Blumenstein, R. Lidor, & G. Tenenbaum (Eds.), *Psychology of sport training* (pp. 62-103). Oxford: Meyer & Meyer Sport.

Serpa, S., & Rodrugues, J. (2001). High performance sports and the experience of human development. In G. Tenenbaum (Ed.), *The practice of sport psychology* (pp. 101-128). Morgantown, WV: Fitness Information Technology.

Statler, T., & Henschen, K. (2009). A sport psychology service delivery model for developing and current track and field athletes and coaches. In T. Hung, R. Lidor, & D. Hackfort (Eds.), *Psychology of Sport Excellence* (pp. 25-31). Mogantown, WV: Fitness Information Technology.

Vealey, R. (2007). Mental skills training in sport. In G. Tenenbaum & R. Eklund (Eds.), *Handbook of sport psychology* (3rd ed., pp. 287-309). Eastbourne, East Sussex: Wiley.

Vernacchia, R. (2003). Working with individual team sports: The psychology of track and field. In R. Lidor & K. Henschen (Eds.), *The psychology of team sports* (pp. 235-262). Morgantown, WV: Fitness Information Technology.

Williams, J. (Ed.). (2001). *Applied sport psychology: personal growth to peak performance* (4th ed.). Mountain View, CA: Mayfield.

Williams, J., & Krane, V. (2001). Psychological characteristics of peak performance. In J. Williams (Ed.), *Applied sport psychology: Personal growth to peak performance* (4th ed., pp. 162-178). Mountain View, CA: Mayfield.

Chapter 2. Psychological Skills for High Performance

This chapter describes psychological aspects of peak performance and the psychological skills required for the best athletic execution in various sports. Today, most athletes and coaches realize the importance of psychological factors during peak performance at major competitions.

Peak performance – The ideal state of body and mind

Peak athletic performances represent those magic moments in which an athlete "puts it all together", both "physically and mentally" (Williams & Krane, 2001, p. 162). Several track and field world record holders who were psychologically trained over the years with the first author reported immediately following their success that "… it was very comfortable; only if I knew that I would set a record I could have performed much better...". Over many years of experience, we have noticed that when athletes are at their "peak performance," many of them also report that they are at a period of high concentration and that they are thinking clearly. Often they cannot hear the coach's remarks from the outside or tune in reactions; their attention is fully devoted to the performance, and most of them emphasize the vital role of psychological factors in their competitions. Bompa (1999) described peaking as the highlight of athletic shape, a special training state which is "characterized by a high CNS adaptation, motor and biological harmony, high motivation, ability to cope with frustration, accepting the implicit risk of competing, and high self-confidence" (p. 95). Indeed, in modern competitions, many strong athletes take part, similarly physically, technically, and tactically prepared, but only those who are the strongest mentally on that given day will win. As best described by Rushall (1989, p. 165) "…psychology is the key to sporting excellence…".

Much research has been carried out in the areas of peak performance (e.g., Cohn, 1991; Garfield & Benett, 1984; Loehr, 1984; Privette & Bundrick, 1997; Ravizza, 1977, 2001), flow state (e.g., Csikszentmihalyi, 1990; Jackson, 2000), and individualized zone of optimal functioning (e.g., Hanin,

2000), enabling us to describe the general profile which is typical of this "ideal body/mind state" (Williams & Krane, 2001) as follows:

- High concentration (appropriately focused)

- Positive preoccupation with the sport event (imagery and thoughts)

- Self-regulation of arousal (energized yet relaxed without stressful distractions)

- High level of self-confidence

- In control, yet relaxed

- Determination and commitment to high performance.

This ideal performance state does not just happen, rather it follows a long and involved process during which athletes have acquired the necessary skills that enable them to cope with competitive stress distractions and to achieve peak athletic performance (Williams & Krane, 2001) (see Figure 2.1).

Figure 2.1. Schematic description of the pathway to victory (a psychological perspective)

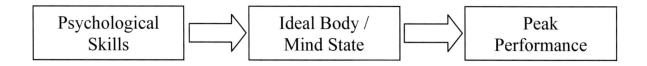

There are a number of psychological skills that are commonly used by elite athletes in their quest to achieve peak performance. These include imagery, goal setting, self-confidence, positive thinking, self-awareness, attentional focus, arousal control, and decision making (Williams & Krane, 2001; Vealey, 2007). Additional psychological skills in various sports types will be discussed below.

<u>Peak performance and psychological skills</u>

During the past three decades sport psychology researchers and applied psychologists have focused on psychological skills that are essential for enhancing athlete performance (Gould, 2002; Gould &

Damarjian, 1998; Henschen, 2005; Orlick & Partington, 1988; Vealey, 1988, 2007). For example, Vealey (1988, 2007) described a model of mental skills for athletes and coaches that include foundation, performance, personal development, and team skills. Gould and Damarjian (1998) focused on learning skills and techniques that enhance elite athletic performance, among them, goal setting, stress management, and confidence enhancement. In addition, there is a particular need to develop codes of ethics, leadership, and goal setting skills in youth athletes.

A series of studies performed by Gould and his colleagues examined significant psychological skills of elite (Olympic champions) sport performance (Gould, Dieffenbach, & Moffett, 2002). These studies revealed that the best elite athletes were characterized by a high level of self-confidence, as well as the ability to cope with and control their anxiety and to focus and block out distractions. Williams and Krane (2001) investigated several specific mental skills that are associated with peak performance. Among these were skills to cope with distractions, concentration, high levels of self-confidence, self-regulation of arousal and goal setting.

Applied psychologists have often discussed the following mental skills for the enhancement of athlete performance:

❖ Relaxation and arousal regulation (e.g., Williams & Harris, 2001; Statler & Henschen, 2009)

❖ Concentration (e.g., Moran, 2003; Vernacchia, 2003)

❖ Goal setting (e.g., Gould, 2001)

❖ Imagery (e.g., Suinn, 1993; Vealey, 1988; Vealey & Greenleaf, 2001)

❖ Self-confidence (e.g., Gould, Dieffenbach, & Moffett, 2002)

❖ Pre-competition mental routines (i.e., Lidor & Singer, 2003; Statler & Henschen, 2009).

The effectiveness of these psychological skills for the enhancement of athletic performance has also been reported in studies by elite practitioners (e.g., Vealey, 2007; Williams & Krane, 2001). The development of mental skills and mental skill profiles for different sports are described below (see Table 2.1). We chose track and field, combat sports, gymnastics, rhythmic gymnastics, canoe/kayak, soccer, basketball, and swimming, since we have a great deal of experience in psychological support and PST with athletes from these sports. our work with these athletes will be described in the Chapter III.

Table 2.1. Examples of recommended psychological skills for several sport types

Sport type	Main psychological skills	Reference
Track and Field (general)	Composure Concentration Confidence	Vernacchia & Statler, 2005
Track and Field (specific) Sprint, Long Distance Running, Jumping, Throwing, Race Walking	Concentration Confidence Self-regulation Visualization Thought control Comfortable pace Motivation	Dosil, 2006b
Combat Sports (general)	Psychological readiness Confidence Self-motivation Creativity Competitiveness	Anshel & Payne, 2006
Judo, Taekwondo	Self-regulation Concentration Anticipation Self-talking	Blumenstein, Lidor, & Tenenbaum, 2005
Gymnastics	Focus Concentration via imagery Confidence building Anxiety control Mental relaxation	Cogan, 2006
Rhythmic Gymnastics	Goal setting Self-talk Self-confidence Attention-focusing via Imagery Mental relaxation Self-awareness	Lidor, Blumenstein, & Tenenbaum, 2007
Kayak / Canoe	Mental control Mental toughness Mental self-regulation Relaxation Focusing	Blumenstein & Bar-Eli, 2001 Blumenstein & Lidor, 2004 Lidor, Blumenstein, & Tenenbaum, 2007
Swimming	Self-regulation of Arousal Confidence Control	Kerr, 2001
Soccer	Concentration Self-regulation Self-talk Positive thinking	Dosil, 2006 Moran, 2003 Lidor, Blumenstein, & Tenenbaum, 2007
Basketball	Imagery Concentration Self-talk Team Cohesion Motivation Self-regulation	Burke, 2006, Burke & Brown, 2003 Henschen & Cook, 2003 Lidor, Blumenstein, & Tenenbaum, 2007

Psychological Skills for Different Sports

Track and field. Following Vernacchia and Statler (2005) and Statler and Henschen (2009), the following skills are of special importance to track and field athletes: composure skills, concentration skills, and confidence skills. However, we understand that sprints, jumps, throws, and long distance runs) are not the same type of events. Each of these has unique psychological characteristics and specific demands. For example, in 100m and 200m sprints, the reaction time constitutes a crucial factor; therefore, the psychological skills emphasized should be concentration and confidence, to improve the swiftness of the start, and to maximize performance during the sprint (Dosil, 2006b). Jumping and throwing events are typified by long breaks between attempts, and thus self-regulation skills, visualization, and thought control, should be strengthened. Long distance events (marathon and race walking) are characterized by long duration of physical effort, and athletes in these events may be confronted with several psychological barriers (e.g., 35 km for marathon, "second" wind, etc.). These psychological traits include concentrating on a "comfortable" running pace, confidence, and composure skills, which should receive special attention during the preparation of these athletes.

Combat sports (judo, wrestling, taekwondo, fencing). While each of these sports has unique characteristics and its own history, all share several psychological skills, such as: psychological readiness, confidence, self-motivation for creativity, and self-regulation to maintain an optimal level of concentration and anticipation (Anshel & Payne, 2006).

One of the characteristics common to Olympic combat situations shared by judo, taekwondo, wrestling, fencing, and boxing is the instantaneous changes occurring within brief time spans (e.g., 100 - 200 msec); accordingly, emotional and mental states may be subjected to extreme and rapid fluctuations during combat fights.

30

Combat sport events share several specific characteristics and requirements of psychological skills. While in a high state of tension when striving to achieve the designated goals, the competing athletes must simultaneously attack and defend, and at the same time conceal their intentions from the opponents It is a challenge to make decisions under time pressure while facing aggressive opponents, and to devise alternative tactical movements such as attention and flexibility (Blumenstein, Bar-Eli, & Collins, 2002; Blumenstein, Lidor, & Tenenbaum, 2005).

Judo requires quick responses, with high levels of attention, self-control, consistency, and will power during the 5-min match (Blumenstein, Lidor & Tenenbaum, 2005; Pedro & Durbin, 2001). Among the psychological traits that are important for judo are confidence, anticipation, concentration, self-talking, and self-control, as well as the skill of self-talking (Anshel & Payne, 2006; Blumenstein, Lidor, & Tenenbaum, 2005) (see Chapter III for more details).

Taekwondo is primarily a self-defense sport, with original foot (70%) and hand techniques (Chung & Lee, 1994). It is a sport of both body and mind during competition, and consists of 3 rounds, with 2 min when fighters fight each other and a 1-min interval between rounds. Park and Seabourne (1997) suggested that one of the key demands in taekwondo is "to achieve a state of mind in which the performer is acutely aware of the endlessly changing competition environment and can effortlessly react to such changes "(p. 14). Among the psychological skills important for taekwondo are self-control, concentration, self-confidence, anticipation, and competitiveness (Anshel & Payne, 2006; Blumenstein, Lidor, & Tenenbaum, 2005).

Individual sports events require distinctive psychological traits that are somewhat different from those described for combat sport.

Artistic gymnastics is characterized by a high degree of mental power compared to other sports, in which there is highly-developed strength, grace, endurance, and persistence (Cogan, 2006). Female gymnastics competitions consist of four events: vault, uneven parallel bars (bars), balance beam

(beam), and floor exercise (floor). Men's gymnastics includes six events: floor, parallel bars, high bar, pommel horse, rings, and vault. Among the main psychological skills required for artistic gymnastics are focus (through imagery), confidence, anxiety control, and mental relaxation (Cogan, 2006);

Rhythmic gymnastics is a sport that combines elements of dance, ballet, and gymnastics, as well as requiring a high level of equipment manipulation. Female rhythmic gymnasts perform a 90-sec routine in which one of five accessories is manipulated: ball, club, hoop, ribbon, and rope. This event requires a demonstration of strength, balance, coordination, and flexibility, as well as a high level of accuracy (Lidor, Blumenstein, & Tenenbaum, 2007). In team performance five gymnasts perform during 2.5 min and exhibit their competitive performance accompanied by music. Rhythmic gymnastics requires the psychological skills of goal setting, self-talk, self-confidence, attention-focusing, mental relaxation, and self-awareness (Lidor, Blumenstein, & Tenenbaum, 2007).

Kayaking is characterized by high endurance and speed, an explosive start, and the maintenance of high speed and tempo throughout the entire distance of the race (Blumenstein & Lidor, 2004; Lidor, Blumenstein, & Tenenbaum, 2007). Studies have shown that mental control, relaxation, mental toughness, focusing, and mental self-regulation are essential psychological skills required for peak performance in kayaking (Blumenstein & Bar-Eli, 2001; Lidor, Blumenstein, & Tenenbaum, 2007).

Success in team sports events necessitates psychological traits that are different from those required for individual sport events.

Soccer field players are required to play in a coordinated defensive and offensive structure (Gray & Drewitt, 1999). To do this, players are expected to master individual defensive (e.g., positioning) and offensive (e.g., dribbling, kicking, and passing) skills, as well as defensive and offensive team skills. The psychological skills important in soccer games include the following: concentration (e.g., Dosil, 2006a; Lidor, Blumenstein, & Tenenbaum, 2007), self-regulation (e.g., Dosil, 2006a; Lidor, Blumenstein, & Tenenbaum, 2007), self-talk (e.g., Lidor, Blumenstein, & Tenenbaum, 2007), and positive thinking (e.g., Lidor, Blumenstein, & Tenenbaum, 2007).

Basketball. In basketball five players play against five opposing players under rapidly changing situations (Wooden, 1980). Basketball players spend a great deal of training time in improving physical abilities such as agility, speed, explosive power, and strength. During a game, players perform a variety of open offensive skills such as dribbling, passing, and shooting; cognitive processes such as anticipation and decision making are applied in defensive maneuvers (Lidor, Blumenstein, & Tenenbaum, 2007). In addition, concentration (Burke, 2006; Burke & Brown, 2003), self-talk (Henschen & Cook, 2003), team cohesion, self-regulation, and motivation (Lidor, Blumenstein, & Tenenbaum, 2007) are required to maximize success in this sport event.

To summarize this section, the following psychological skills are typically used in different sports to achieve peak performance:

- ❖ Self-regulation of arousal
- ❖ Concentration
- ❖ Confidence
- ❖ Self-talk.

These commonalities in psychological skills are derived from the results of numerous studies of peak performance and from practitioners' reports. However, it should be emphasized that each sport has unique demands for psychological skills that may guarantee peak performance in this sport. Accordingly, Williams and Krane (2001) report that peak performance is "...a product of the body and mind, and it can be trained. Just as improving physical skills, strategies, and conditioning increases the likelihood of peak performance, learning to control psychological readiness and the ideal mental climate for peak performance also enhances performance" (p. 175-176).

Psychological Skills and Mental Training Techniques

Traditional mental training techniques that have been widely used for psychological skills development include relaxation/arousal regulation, biofeedback training, imagery, goal setting, concentration, self-talk, and a pre-competitive mental routine (Henschen, 2005; Vealey, 2007). Unfortunately, most elite athletes do not make use of these techniques during their training (Frey, Laguna, & Ravizza, 2003). However, numerous research studies and evidence in practical experience have shown the effectiveness of mental training techniques on psychological skills development (Vealey, 2007).

Relaxation is a very popular technique in sport, and may be useful in helping athletes regulate their energy use in order to allow peak performance (Vealey, 2007). Moreover, it has been reported that proper application of relaxation techniques may facilitate recovery from exercise (Vealey, 2007), this is particularly important in instances where athletes have only a short pause between fights or starts, or when they are fatigued.

The ability to regulate physical energy or arousal levels is widely regarded as an important mental skill in sport (Gould & Udry, 1994). Not surprisingly, relaxation skills must be practiced on a systematic basis like any traditional athletic training processes.

The most popular and well-known relaxation techniques are "muscle-to–mind" techniques, such as breathing exercises, and progressive muscular relaxation introduced by Jacobson (1930), and other "mind-to-muscle" techniques such as autogenic training (Schultz, 1932), meditation, yoga, and hypnosis. These techniques have been widely described in numerous handbooks and instruction manuals (e.g., Henschen, 2005; Williams & Harris, 2001) and are extensively used in sport psychology practice.

Relaxation techniques are commonly used for recovery at the end of a practice day in rhythmic gymnastics, judo, fencing, soccer, basketball; between fights in combat sports; and ,as part of warm-up in track and field, swimming, shooting, etc. Moreover, relaxation is applied as a method to accelerate practice the day before competition. For example, we observed that biofeedback training and relaxation significantly enhanced athletic performance in a 100 m dash (Blumenstein, Bar-Eli & Tenenbaum, 1995).

Imagery is a popular mental training technique used by athletes (Morris, Spittle, & Watt, 2005). Application of this technique prior to competition was reported to improve performance (Vealey & Greenleaf, 2006), facilitate competition preparation (Morris et al., 2005), and enhance physical, perceptual, and psychological skills (Vealey & Greenleaf, 2006).

Imagery has been incorporated into many different PST and models, such as visual-motor behavior rehearsal (VMBR; Suinn, 1984), the five-step strategy (Singer, 1988), and the Wingate five-step approach (Blumenstein et al., 2002). Although the use of imagery may facilitate athletic performance, in practice, similar to physical training, acquiring the psychological skill of imagery requires systematic practice.

During our long experience imagery was used as part of the athletes' pre-competitive routine in swimming, track and field, rhythmic gymnastics, windsurfing, basketball, and shooting. Moreover, we combined imagery with relaxation and biofeedback training in a laboratory setting to build up athletes' technical-tactical abilities in judo, fencing, taekwondo, basketball, and gymnastics (see Chapter III for more details).

Concentration refers to the ability of the athlete to focus and devote full attention on a specific task, and not be distracted or affected by irrelevant exterior and inner stimuli (Moran, 1996). Concentration skill is often the key factor in athletic performance and competition. According to Nideffer (1989), there are several concentration styles that all athletes should possess. These include: broad external, narrow internal, narrow external, broad internal, shifting. The concentration style that is applied is individually determined by the different sports and sport situations, the individual's ability to effectively concentrate, physiological arousal states, etc.

In order to develop concentration skills in applied sport psychology, we recommend the use of several techniques, such as:

- Goal setting ("performance goals") – focuses the mind on realistic task-relevant thoughts
- Pre-competitive (pre-performance) routines – the athlete is trained to concentrate only on what can controlled
- Imagery – helps athlete to rehearse their goals
- Self-talk ("triggers") – trains the athlete to re-focus quickly on task-relevant cues
- Arousal control – relaxes body awareness
- Biofeedback training – help athlete to concentrate on their behavior based on instantaneous audio-visual physiological responses.

We have been using these techniques widely in the laboratory and in field situations in different sports events, including rhythmic gymnastics, combat sports, basketball, soccer, shooting, tennis, swimming, and track and field.

Self-talk is another technique in which athletes individually evaluate a given situation by a verbal dialogue providing self-instructions or reinforcement. Negative self-talk often leads to anxiety or to depression commonly associated with training and competition (Henschen, 2005). However, positive self-talk may be effective in enhancing different types of sport performance (Hatzigeorgiadis, Theodorakis, & Zourbanos, 2004).

We made it clear to the athletes that our mind controls our body, and the manner in which we think and talk to ourselves in our minds dictates the directions that our bodies will follow. Therefore, we recommend that they athletes remain in the present, use positive cues or trigger-words, and focus on their short-term and long-term goals, and in doing so their bodies will follow their thoughts.

Pre-competition performance routines bring together the applications of all the mental skills into a sport routine that will enhance athletic performance. A mental routine is unique to each athlete, and is made up of a combination of a number of mental skills (Henschen, 2005). Various aspects of pre-performance routines have been reported by sports scientists and applied sport psychologists (e.g., Singer, Hausenblas, & Jannelle, 2001; Lidor & Singer, 2003). The routine becomes an integral element of the athlete's repertoire in preparation for various competitions. Among the effects of a well-developed pre-performance routine are improving concentration, preventing negative thoughts, blocking out external distractions, and developing a plan of action before the performance begins (Moran, 1996). Examples of psychological routines in tennis, athletics, basketball and soccer were described by Samulski and Lopes (2008).

Chapter III will deliberate on integrating and implementing several psychological skills in typical training programs during the athlete's training process.

References

Anshel, M., & Payne, M. (2006). Application of sport psychology for optimal performance in martial arts. In J. Dosil (Ed.), *The sport psychologist's handbook: A guide for sport-specific performance enhancement* (pp. 353-374). Chichester, UK: Wiley.

Blumenstein, B., & Bar-Eli, M. (2001). A five-step approach for biofeedback in sport. *Sportwissenschaft*, *4*, 412-424.

Blumenstein, B., & Lidor, R. (2004). Psychological preparation in elite canoeing and kayaking sport programs: Periodization and planning. *Applied Research in Coaching and Athletics Annual*, *19*, 24-34.

Blumenstein, B., Bar-Eli, M., & Collins, D. (2002). Biofeedback training in sport. In *Brain and body in sport and exercise: Biofeedback applications in performance enhancement* (pp. 55-76). Chichester, UK: Wiley.

Blumenstein, B., Bar-Eli, M., & Tenenbaum, G. (1995). The augmenting role of biofeedback: Effects of autogenic training, imagery and music on physiological indices and athletic performance. *Journal of Sport Sciences, 13,* 343-354.

Blumenstein, B., Lidor, R., & Tenenbaum, G. (2005). Periodization and planning of psychological preparation in elite combat sport programs: The case of judo. *International Journal of Sport and Exercise Psychology*, *3*, 7-25.

Bompa, T. (1999). *Theory and methodology of training* (3rd ed.). Dubuque, IA: Kendall/Hunt.

Burke, K. (2006). Using sport psychology to improve basketball performance. In J. Dosil (Ed.), *The sport psychologist's handbook: A guide for sport-specific performance enhancement* (pp. 121-138). Chichester, UK: Wiley.

Burke, K., & Brown, D. (2003). *Sport psychology library series: Basketball.* Morgantown, WV: Fitness Information Technology.

Chung, K., & Lee, K. (1994). *Taekwondo kyorugi: Olympic style sparring.* Hartford, CT: Turtle Press.

Cogan, K. (2006). Sport psychology in gymnastics. In J. Dosil (Ed.), *The sport psychologist's handbook: A guide for sport-specific performance enhancement* (pp. 641-661). Chichester, UK: Wiley.

Cohn, D. (1991). An exploratory study on peak performance in golf. *The Sport Psychologist, 5,* 1-14.

Csikszentmihalyi, M. (1990). *Flow: The psychology of optimal experience.* New York: Harper & Row.

Dosil, J. (2006a). Psychological interventions with football (soccer) teams. In J. Dosil (Ed.), *The sport psychologist's handbook: A guide for sport-specific performance enhancement* (pp. 139-158). Chichester, UK: Wiley.

Dosil, J. (2006b). The psychology of athletics. In J. Dosil (Ed.), *The sport psychologist's handbook: A guide for sport-specific performance enhancement* (pp. 265-284). Chichester, UK: Wiley.

Frey, M., Laguna, P., & Ravizza, K. (2003). Collegiate athlete's mental skill use and perceptions of success: An exploration of the practice and competition settings. *Journal of Applied Sport Psychology,* 15:115-128.

Garfield, C., & Benett, H. (1984). *Peak performance: Mental training techniques of the world's greatest athletes.* Los Angeles: Tarcher.

Gould, D. (2001). Goal setting for peak performance. In J. Williams (Ed.), *Applied sport psychology: Personal growth to peak performance* (4th ed., pp. 190-205). Mountain View, CA: Mayfield.

Gould, D. (2002). The psychology of Olympic excellence and its development. *Psychology, 9,* 531-546.

Gould, D., & Damarjian, N. (1998). Mental skills training in sport. In B. Elliot (Ed.), *Applied sport science: Training in sport. International Handbook of Sport Science* (Vol. 3, pp. 69-116). Sussex, England: Wiley.

Gould, D., & Udry, E. (1994). Psychological skills for enhancing performance: Arousal regulating strategies. *Medicine and Science in Sport and Exercise, 26,* 478-485.

Gould, D., Deiffenbach, K., & Moffett, A. (2002). Psychological characteristics and their development in Olympic champions. *Journal of Applied Sport Psychology, 14,* 177-209.

Gray, A., & Drewitt, J. (1999). *Flat back four – The tactical game.* London: Boxfree.

Hanin, Y. (2000). Individual zones of optimal functioning (IZOF) model: Emotion-performance relationships in sport. In Y. Hanin (Ed.), *Emotions in sport* (pp. 65-89). Champaign, IL: Human Kinetics.

Hatzigeorgiadis, A., Theordorakis, Y., & Zourbanos, N. (2004). Self-talk in the swimming pool: The effects of self-talk on thought content and performance in water-polo tasks. *Journal of Applied Sport Psychology, 16,* 138-150.

Henschen, K. (2005). Mental practice – Skill oriented. In D. Hackfort, J. Duda, & R. Lidor (Eds.), *Handbook of research in applied sport and exercise psychology: International perspectives* (pp. 19-36). Morgantown, WV: Fitness Information Technology.

Henschen, K., & Cook, D. (2003). Working with professional basketball players. In R. Lidor & K. Henschen (Eds.), *The psychology of team sports* (pp. 143-160). Morgantown, WV: Fitness Information Technology.

Jackson, S. (2000). Joy, fun and flow state in sport. In Y. Hanin (Ed.), *Emotions in sport* (pp. 135-156). Champaign, IL: Human Kinetics.

Jacobson, E. (1930). *Progressive relaxation.* Chicago: University of Chicago Press.

Kerr, B. (2001). Community-based sport psychology. In G. Tenenbaum (Ed.), *The practice of sport psychology* (pp. 155-167). Morgantown, WV: Fitness Information Technology.

Lidor, R., & Singer, R. (2003). Preperformance routines in self-paced tasks: Developmental and educational considerations. In R. Lidor & K. Henschen (Eds.), *The psychology of team sports* (pp. 69-98). Morgantown, WV: Fitness Information Technology.

Lidor, R., & Singer, R. (2003). Preperformance routines in self-paced tasks: Development and educational considerations. In R. Lidor & K. Henschen (Eds.), *The psychology of team sports* (pp. 69-98). Morgantown, WV: Fitness Information Technology.

Lidor, R., Blumenstein, B., & Tenenbaum, G. (2007). Periodization and planning of psychological preparation in individual and team sports. In B. Blumenstein, R. Lidor, G. Tenenbaum (Eds.), *Psychology of Sport Training* (pp. 137-161). Oxford, UK: Meyer & Meyer Sports.

Loehr, J. (1984). How to overcome stress and play at your peak all the time. *Tennis*, 66-76.

Moran, A. (1996). *The psychology of concentration in sport performers: A cognitive analysis.* East Sussex, UK: Psychology Press.

Moran, A. (2003). Improving concentration skills in team-sport performance: Focusing techniques for soccer players. In R. Lidor & K. Henschen (Eds.), *The psychology of team sports* (pp. 161-190). Morgantown, WV: Fitness Information Technology.

Morris, T., Spittle, M., & Watt, A. (2005). *Imagery in sport.* Champaign, IL: Human Kinetics.

Nideffer, R. (1989). *Attention control training for sport.* Los Gatos, CA: Enhanced Performance Service.

Orlik, T., & Partington, J. (1988). Mental links to excellence. *The Sport Psychologist, 2,* 105-130.

Park, Y., & Seabourne, T. (1997). *Taekwondo techniques and tactics.* Champaign, IL: Human Kinetics.

Pedro, J., & Durbin, W. (2001). *Judo: Techniques and tactics.* Champaign, IL: Human Kinetics.

Privette, G., & Bundrick, C. (1997). Psychological process of peak, average, and tailing performance in sport. *International Journal of Sport Psychology, 28,* 323-334.

Ravizza, K. (1977). Peak experiences in sport. *Journal of Humanistic Psychology, 17*, 35-40.

Ravizza, K. (2001). Reflections and insights from the field on performance enhancement

consultation. In G. Tenenbaum (Ed.), *The practice of sport psychology* (pp. 197-216).

Morgantown, WV: Fitness Information Technology.

Rushall, B.S. (1989). Sport psychology: The key to sporting excellence. *International Journal of*

Sport Psychology, 20, 165-190.

Samulski, D., & Lopes, M. (2008). Counseling Brazilian athletes during the Olympic Games in

Athens 2004: Important issues and intervention techniques. *International Journal of Sport*

and Exercise Psychology, 6, 277-286.

Schultz, J. (1932). Das autogene Training (Autogenic Training), Stuttgart: Thieme.

Singer, R. (1988). Strategies and metastrategies in learning and performing self-paced athletic skills.

Sport Psychologist, 2, 49-68.

Singer, R., Hausenblas, H., & Janelle, C. (Eds.). (2000). *Handbook of Sport psychology* (2nd ed.).

New York: Wiley.

Statler, T., & Henschen, K. (2009). A sport psychology service delivery model for developing and

current track and field athletes and coaches. In T. Hung, R. Lidor, & D. Hackfort (Eds.),

Psychology of sport excellence (pp. 25-31). Morgantown, WV: Fitness Information

Technology.

Suinn, R. (1984). Imagery and sports. In W. Straub & J. Williams (Eds.), *Cognitive sport*

psychology (pp. 253-272). Lansing, NY: Sport Science Associates.

Suinn, R. (1993). Imagery. In R. Singer, M. Murphey, & L. Tennant (Eds.), *Handbook of research*

on sport psychology (p. 492-510). New York: Macmillan.

Vealey, R. (1988). Future directions in psychological skills training. *Sport Psychology, 2,* 318-336.

Vealey, R. (2007). Mental skills training in sport. In G. Tenenbaum & R. Eklund (Eds.), *Handbook*

of sport psychology (3rd ed., pp. 287-309). New York: Wiley.

Vealey, R., & Greenleaf, C. (2001). Seeing is believing: Understanding and using imagery in sport. In J. Williams (Ed.), *Applied sport psychology: Personal growth to peak performance* (4th ed., pp. 247-283). Mountain View, CA: Mayfield.

Vealey, R., & Greenleaf, C. (2006). Seeing is believing: Understanding and using imagery in sport. In J. Williams (Ed.), *Applied sport psychology: Personal growth to peak performance* (5th ed., pp. 306-348). Boston: McGraw-Hill.

Vernacchia, R. (2003). Working with individual team sports: The psychology of track and field. In R. Lidor & K. Henschen (Eds.), *The psychology of team sports* (pp. 235-265). Morgantown, WV: Fitness Information Technology.

Vernacchia, R., & Statler, T. (2005). *The psychology of high performance track and field.* Mountain View, CA: Track and Field News.

Williams, J., & Harris, D. (2001). Relaxation and energizing techniques for regulation of arousal. In J. Williams (Ed.), *Applied sport psychology: Personal growth to peak performance* (4th ed., pp. 229-246). Mountain View, CA: Mayfield.

Williams, J., & Krane, V. (2001). Psychological characteristics of peak performance. In J. Williams (Ed.), *Applied sport psychology: Personal growth to peak performance* (4th ed., pp. 162-178). Mountain View, Mayfield.

Wooden, J. (1980). *Practical modern basketball* (2nd ed.). New York: Wiley.

Chapter 3. Psychological Skills Training Programs for Performance Enhancement

Psychological skills training (PST), or "mental skills training", refers to techniques and strategies designed to "teach or enhance mental skills that facilitate performance and a positive approach to sport competition" (Vealey, 1988, p. 319). Techniques and strategies for psychological interventions to improve athletic performance include training of arousal regulation, imagery, self-talk, goal-setting, and concentration (Blumenstein, Lidor, & Tenenbaum, 2007; Gould & Damarjian, 1998; Henschen, 2005; Moran, 2005; Vealey, 2007; Weinberg & Williams, 2001). Sport psychology researchers have worked intensively to establish a data base concerning the effectiveness of different psychological interventions in improving performance (e.g., Duran-Bush & Salmela, 2002; Greenspan & Feltz, 1989; Vealey, 1994, 2007).

Our current knowledge teaches us that an effective psychological intervention must be carried out in an individualized, systematic manner, over time, It and should be integrated with physical training and employ a variety of psychological techniques as part of the training program (see Blumenstein et al., 2007; Dosil, 2006; Gould & Carson, 2007; Vealey, 2007; Weinberg & Williams, 2001).

Several PST programs in different sports will be discussed below. We recommend that typical PST training processes should follows our approach, which is discussed below.

The philosophical basis of our approach. According to Vealey (2007), three main approaches are used in PST: 1) the educational versus clinical approach 2) the program-centered versus athlete-centered approach, and 3) the performance enhancement versus personal development approach. Weinberg and Williams (2001) noted in their research the clinical and educational-philosophical approaches used by sport psychologists. However, research and experience both indicate that most athletes benefit more from an educational rather than a clinical approach (Morris & Thomas, 1995).

The educational approach, which is based on athletes' learning skills, is closer to athletes because it shares the same educational processes that the athletes experience during the training practice.

We will now discuss some points of the educational approach founded on our experience with applied field intervention where we learned that during physical training and competitions, the athlete expects immediate feedback. Thus, during mental training sessions in most psychological and intervention programs, there should be a link between goal setting, immediate feedback, and performance (See Figure 3.1).

Figure 3.1. Suggested link between intervention, immediate feedback, and performance for most mental sessions

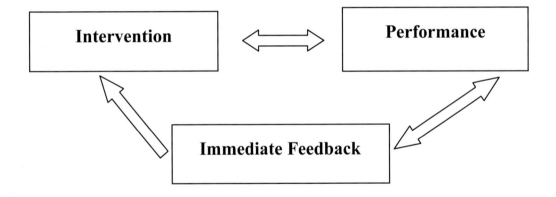

❖ In order to make the mental training applicable, there is a need to develop a specific individual set of criteria and norms for mental performance. These include speed, accuracy, and stability (reliability).

❖ It is recommended that some of the mental training sessions include psycho-motor exercises in which psychological skills are closely associated with sport-specific tasks, for example concentration and reaction time in combat sport, or relaxation, concentration, and imagery in rhythmic sport gymnastics.

46

❖ In the process of preparing for actual competition (real-life situations), the athlete is instructed to perform at various levels of difficulty, or under simulated real-life distractions that typically occur during competitions. Therefore, we have devised a specific scale of variable difficulty levels that the athlete is expected to successfully complete, to assure that his/her ability to cope with real-life situations will improve (see Table 3.1).

Table 3.1. Stress factor scale simulating varying distraction (difficulty) levels typical of real-life situations (i.e. competitions)

Difficulty Level	Description
1	Ordinary laboratory settings
2	Verbal motivation (positive/negative)
3	Performance under precise demands – graded (performance) perfection levels
4	Reward / punishment for performance
5	Performance under "true" competition noise (competition audio clips)
6	Performance under "true" competition sights (competition video clips)
7	Various combinations of levels 1-6

Level 1. Consists of 5-10 sessions, provided in ordinary laboratory settings (learning segments).

Level 2. Consists of 7-8 sessions, provided with negative and positive verbal comments during mental performances (i.e., concentration exercises with positive verbal comments such as "great" and "you are a star", or negative comments such as "you are unstable today" and "this is not your day").

Level 3. Mental performance with specific demands, such as a time limit (e.g., 5, 10, or 20 sec of concentration exercises); performance with a well-defined outcome (e.g., rapidly performing a motor task in 160 msec, etc.).

Level 4. Success in a Level 3 performance is rewarded, failure is penalized.

Level 5. Performance while competition sound clips are played.

Level 6. Performance while opponents and self video competition clips are displayed.

Level 7. Combinations of levels 1-6, beginning with level 1 and continue with level shuffles, dynamically defined by current conditions

Levels 1-2 are comprised of 10-15 introductory sessions and are provided during general preparation; levels 3-4 include 15-20 basic sessions and are provided during specific preparation; levels 5-7 are comprised of 10-15 simulation sessions that are provided during the competition phase. The entire procedure should be applied over a 5-6 months period.

PST is a long, continuous process during which there has to be mutual trust between the athlete, coach, and the sport psychologist/consultant. We therefore recommend that the 5-step PST detailed in Table 3.2, and described below, be faithfully followed.

Table 3.2 . Five steps of a psychological skill training (PST) program

I	II	III	IV	V
				Evaluation and correction of PST according to competition outcome
			Develop/Modify competition behavior **skills**; evaluation during competitions	
		PST in laboratory; **Observation** of PST effects during physical training and competitions		
	Diagnosis at laboratory settings; observations of several physical performance sessions and 1-2 competitions			
Meeting with athlete, coach and sport psychologist; Define problems				

Step 1. The first meeting with the coach and the athlete is the key to a fruitful outcome. In this step relationship between the sport psychology consultant, athlete, and coach is established, problems are presented and discussed, and the PST program is described. At this point, it is crucial that the sport psychology consultant understands sports, pays attention to coach and athlete, and finally be capable of clearly describing the PST program.

Step 2. The Diagnosis of individual differences (psychometric data) consists of brief questionnaires and tests, including the STAI (Spielberger, Gorsuch, & Luchene, 1970), SCAT (Martens, Vealey & Burton, 1990), TAIS (Nideffer, 1989); RTP test (Blumenstein, Lidor & Tenenbaum, 2005), SRT (Blumenstein, Bar-Eli, & Collins, 2002), and concentration tests with BFB (Blumenstein & Orbach, in press).

Step 3. PST is provided under laboratory settings paying attention to issues related to psychometric data presented in Steps 1 and 2. PST effects on performance during physical training and competitions were obeservered.

Step 4. The content of mental training sessions is corrected and modified according to the various feedbacks, observations, and athlete-coach comments.

Step 5. Upcoming PST sessions are evaluated and modified.

Planning and periodization in PST

The PST program has become an integral part of training programs in individual and team sports (see Blumenstein et al., 2007; Dosil, 2006). Each of the training phases (preparation, competition, and transition) has its own characteristics and objectives. Therefore, PST programs should take these peculiarities into account (Blumenstein et al., 2007).

- The main goal for PST programs in the **General preparation (GP)** is to learn/improve concentration, relaxation, self-talk, and imagery, and to achieve high levels of sport motivation and self-confidence. Mental sessions are provided 1-2 times per week in

50

laboratory settings following levels 1-2 of the "stress scale" (see Table 3.1), and each session lasts 40-50 minutes.

- The main goals for PST programs during the **Specific preparation** (SP) are to perform psychological skills rapidly and to show stability in situations at levels 3-4 of the "stress factor scale" presented in Table 3.1. Mental sessions are provided 1-3 times per week in lab settings and last 40-50 minutes.

- The main goal for PST programs in the **Competition phase** is to perform psychological skills at levels 5-7 of the "stress scale" (see Table 3.1) with, accuracy and stability. Mental sessions are provided 2-3 times per week in laboratory and also training settings and last 35-45 minutes.

In this chapter we will discuss several sports disciplines (judo, taekwondo, pole vault, rhythmic gymnastics, soccer, and basketball) in which we gained a great deal of experience working with elite athletes, Olympic, World, and European medalists and champions. PST programs were applied as a part of those athletes' training programs.

Psychological techniques and strategies in PST

PST is the systematic employment of procedures that can readily and effectively optimize the athlete's mental and cognitive ability during major athletic events (Gould & Damarjian, 1998). Indeed, "psychological skills are learned and therefore need to be practiced systematically, just like physical skills" (Weinberg & Williams, 2001, p. 352).

The effectiveness of PST has been supported across several research projects and numerous practitioners' examples (e.g., Gould & Carson, 2007; Vealey, 2007).

Relaxation, imagery, self-talk, concentration, biofeedback training, and goal setting are the main techniques/strategies currently being used in PST to enhance performance. These techniques are helping athletes to cope with stress, develop an optimal arousal level, focus attention on the task, develop motivation for training and competition, and improve self-confidence (Morris & Thomas, 1995; Vealey, 2007; Weinberg & Williams, 2001).

During mental training sessions several psychological techniques may be grouped in a "package" of strategies. The strategies in psychological skills training may include:

- ❖ 5-SA – Five-Step Approach (Singer, 1988)
- ❖ W5SA – Wingate Five Step Approach to mental training using biofeedback (Blumenstein, Bar-Eli, & Tenenbaum, 2002)
- ❖ UMBR – Visuo-motor behavioral rehearsal (Suinn, 1993)
- ❖ P^3 thinking and goal mapping (Vealey, 2005)
- ❖ Competition focus plan (Orlick, 1986).

The effectiveness of these techniques and strategies, and their assessment in PST, are an important part of the sport psychologist's work, together with the type of sport, the sport psychologist's experience, the concrete defined program, and the specific situation (see Blumenstein et al., 2007; Dosil, 2006; Vealey, 2007; Weinberg & Williams, 2001).

Several examples of integrating and implementing psychological techniques and strategies in various sports will be presented below.

PST in different sports: Integration into training programs

One of the main aims of PST is to improve psychological skills and immediately integrate them with physical skills practice and competition. However, this process is not a quick one, and requires patience. Based on our experience, it follows that athletes prefer to use new skills immediately after several mental training sessions, but only after 3-4 months of PST do they really feel in what way or in what training phase they can apply their psychological skills. A few examples of integrating PST in different sports are discussed below.

Combat sports (judo, taekwondo, wrestling, fencing) are typified by rapid responses, as well as by high levels of attention, self-control, consistency, and will power (Pedro & Durbin, 2001). Situations in competition matches may often change within extremely short periods of time (i.e., 100 to 200 msec); accordingly, emotional and mental states are subject to extreme fluctuations during combat matches. It is difficult for athletes to simultaneously attack and defend while concealing their intentions from their opponent and during extreme states of tension. It is not easy to make decisions under time pressure while facing aggressive opponents and to decide on alternative tactical movements (i.e., attention, flexibility), all while striving to achieve the designated goals (Blumenstein et al., 2005; Pedro & Durbin, 2001).

Some of the most important performance characteristics in combat sports are rapid reflexes, quick reactions, good concentration, and a high level of decision-making. Accordingly, Blumenstein and his colleagues (2005) developed a reaction-training program (RTP) for combat sport. RTP consists of three reactions time (RT) tasks:

1. Simple RT (1 stimulus, 1 response)
2. Two-choice RT (2 stimuli, 2 responses)
3. Discrimination RT (2 stimuli, 1 response).

Motor Tasks: General description. A computer simulation setting was utilized to improve the elite combat athletes' responses (Blumenstein et al., 2005). The athlete was instructed to stand in front of the computer monitor at a distance of 1m. The computer was situated on an office desk (height 80 cm). The athlete followed the instructions presented verbally by the trainer. Specific manipulations were introduced for each task. Each of the tasks proceeded as follows: (a) an empty circle (O) appears at various spots on the PC monitor and a warning message is displayed for 300 msec, (b) a variable delay is presented for 1-2 sec, (c) the circle is filled in (•) (e.g., a stimulus

53

onset), (d) the athlete responds, (e) an inter-trial interval for about 2 sec is allowed, and (f) the procedure starts over.

Simple RT. In this task, one stimulus was presented and one response was required. The response key used in this task was the "Y" key. To begin the task, the athlete placed the right index finger on the "Y" key, without pressing it. An empty circle and a warning message were presented on the monitor for 500 msec to caution that the stimulus would appear shortly. As soon as the circle was filled in (i.e., the stimulus), the athlete had to press the "Y" key as rapidly as possible without making any errors.

Two-choice RT. In this task there were 2 stimuli and 2 responses/choices. To initiate the task, the athlete placed the left index finger on the "T" key, and the right index finger on the "Y" key, without pressing the keys. Two empty circles and a warning message appeared at the center of the monitor for 500 msec to signal that the stimulus would appear soon. If the left circle was filled in, the athlete had to press the "T" key; if the right circle was filled in, the athlete had to press the "Y" key. The athlete was instructed to react as rapidly as possible without making any errors.

Discrimination RT. In this task, there were 2 stimuli but only one response. Two empty circles and a warning message appeared at the center of the monitor for 500 msec to warn that a stimulus would follow shortly. If the left circle was filled in, the athlete had to press the "Y" key with his or her dominant hand as quickly as possible without making any errors.

The athlete performed the three RT tasks in a standing position close to the computer. The athlete was instructed to work freely, quickly, and to be focused on the task.

Sets of Training. Different sets of responses were introduced to the elite combat athlete. Sets of 15 simple RTs, 30 choice RTs, and 30 discrimination RTs were used for the basic program introduced during the GP and SP. It took the elite combat athletes about 5-6 min to complete the basic set of responses, corresponding to match durations of Judo (5 min) and taekwondo (3X2min). During the

SP and competition phases, stress factors were used to increase the psychological load of the athletes while performing the tasks. Norms that were obtained from elite athletes (an Olympic medal holder and four World and six European champions, two youth Olympic medals, and two world Universiada medals) were used to evaluate the quality of the responses made by the elite combat athletes. We observed that in combat sport the time limit for "fast" RT was <200 msec and for "slow" RT >200 msec. It is important to consider the balance between slow and fast RT, as this balance point can serve as a good indication of performance goal. For example, a process was initiated with a 2-3/12-13 ratio (2-3 fast and 12-13 slow RT); following 1-2 months of training, the athlete achieved an 8/7 ratio (8 fast and 7 slow RT) or 10/5 ratio; right before the competition a 14/1 ratio or even 15/0 ratio was recorded. This was a very high quality exercise, which was well correlated with the combat athlete's top quality performance.

Stress Factors Used During Training Sessions. Several stress factors were used, particularly during the SP and competition phases (also see Table 3.1). The following are some of the recommended working protocols we normally apply while working with elite athletes. The response tasks are performed under the following situations:

(a) "Positive" motivation statements are provided, such as "good work," "today is your day," "you are great," and "you can do it."

(b) "Negative" motivation statements are provided, such as "you are having a bad day," "you are weak-willed today," "what are you doing?", and "the referee is against you."

(c) A video demo clip is played simultaneously; for example, competition clips are presented showing specific situations, such as winning and losing, while competing against "easy" and "tough" opponents, or external distractions, such as recordings of competition noises, etc. (see Blumenstein et al., 2005).

(d) The time allocated for the response is restricted; the times of RTs should not exceed the bandwidth of 160-165 msec for a simple RT, 170-175 msec for choice RT, and 165-170 msec for discrimination RT.

(e) A "consequence" phase is introduced to increase awareness, such as 10 sit-ups following an error in key selection or a response slower than the time allocated.

(f) Distractions, such as light hits, are introduced by another athlete using physical contact.

(g) Revealed or hidden results are presented; in the first instance, the athlete is informed about scores, thus knowledge of the results (KR) is provided, and in the second instance, the athlete does not receive KR and totally relies on internal feedback to evaluate his/her own performance.

(h) A self-talk technique is utilized simultaneously; the athlete is instructed to provide running comments related to performances, statements like "it was easy," "it's not so difficult," "I can do it," and "I'm going to make it."

Combinations with Other Psychological Techniques. During PST sessions combat athletes train with relaxation and imagery incorporating biofeedback, along with the response-selection procedure. For example, the athlete performs relaxation with biofeedback for 5 min, followed by a 5 min imagery period. The athlete then performs a set of 15-30-30 RTs in a time limit of 155-175-165 msec, respectively. Another combination used is a set of 15-30-30 RTs in a time limit of 155-175-165 msec, respectively, followed by a 5 min relaxation session and by 15 min of relaxation-excitation biofeedback training. The RTs combinations used and the time limits imposed are unchanged; however, the difference is due to the relaxation conditions provided to the athletes.

Periodization and Loads in the Training Sessions. During the GP phase, athletes usually undergo a large training volume, high physical loads, and numerous repetitions of strength training. In this period, typically lasting between 3-4 months, different relaxation and mental recovery techniques are utilized, such as listening to music and relaxation incorporating biofeedback. The response sets that are given to the athletes are in large volumes. For example, sets of 30-60-60 RTs twice a week or 15-30-30 RTs twice a week are practiced. No feedback schedules are given during the first four weeks of the training program. Approximate results should be about 165-175-170 msec for the simple, choice, and discrimination RTs, respectively. These results were obtained from our long experience with elite athletes during the GP and SP phases of the program, and we used these scores as performance norms in our psychological training program.

In the second and third months, when feedback is given to the athlete, the time target is 160-175-170 msec for the RT tasks; however, pressure factors such as "positive" and "negative" statements (i.e., situations "a" and "b" from section "Stress factors used during training sessions") are also introduced. That is, the athlete is required to demonstrate a similar level of response proficiency under attention-distracted conditions. The athlete is taught to ignore environmental distractions and concentrate solely on the pressing task.

During RT performance the athlete is instructed to follow precise behavior patterns during pauses between reactions, including relaxation followed by concentration followed by motor readiness in preparation for the next reaction (Figure 3.2).

Figure 3.2. Behavior patterns during pause between reactions.

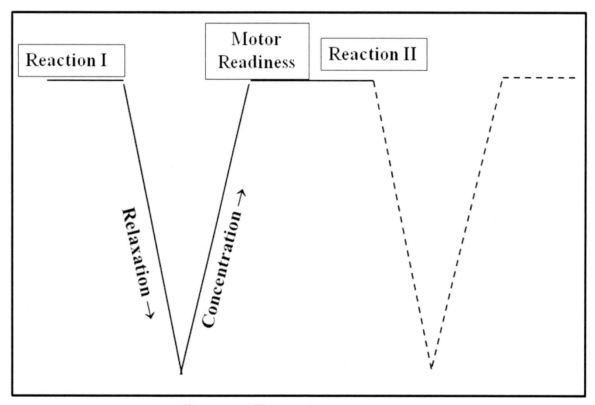

Pattern Duration

Elite combat athletes carry out this behavior pattern rapidly; pauses duration may be altered between 2 or 3 sec. This maneuver has important applications for competitive fights. During the SP phase, athletes participate in numerous training matches with the goals of developing competition strategies to use against potential opponents, and enhancing their technical and tactical capabilities. The psychological training program assists the athletes to be ready for specific competition situations. Therefore, stress factors are introduced to the athletes on a regular basis. During this period, the athletes perform sets of 15-30-30 or 10-20-20 of the response tasks in time limits of 155-170-165 msec, respectively. Different stress factors are used in each training session. We highly recommend the use of video to assist the athletes in recognizing the strengths and weaknesses of potential opponents whom they will be competing against in upcoming international tournaments. In particular, the athletes should closely watch video clip segments of actual combats, and then perform the sets of RT tasks. This method exposes the athlete to visual and noise distractions typical of real combat events.

During the competition phase, the athletes should maintain the value of their response times, and some of them are able to further decrease those values (i.e., respond faster). For example, during the last training session in this stressful phase, the best athletes performed the simple RT in 142±47 msec, with 13 fast and 2 slow (13/2 ratio); the two-choice RT in 140±60 msec with 12/3 ratio (dominant right), and the discrimination RT in 151±40 msec with 14/1 ratio. Most of the athletes reported that they felt confident and aggressive, and that they were not afraid of the upcoming competition (see Figure 3.3).

Figure 3.3. Example of reaction training program (RTP) session.

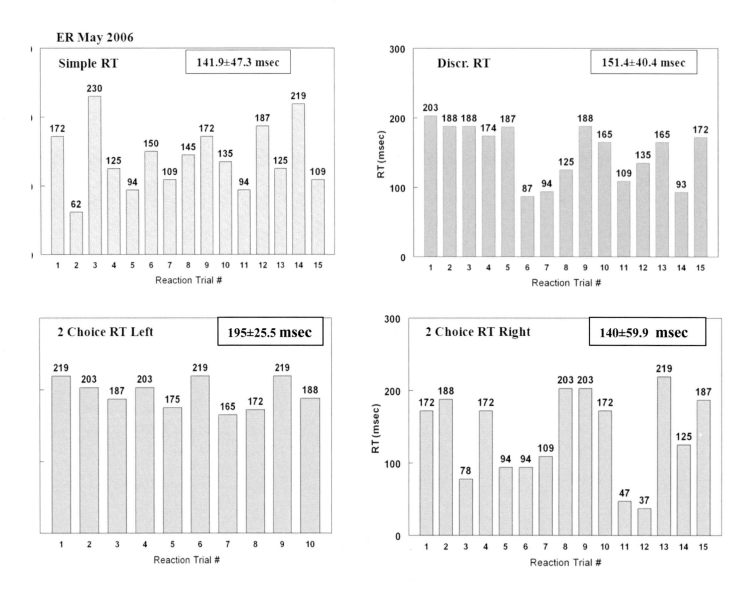

The following case may best illustrate the effectiveness of the program on the judoka's confidence and performance. On the evening before the 2000 Olympic judo tournament began, we applied the response program to one of the judokas, at his request. He performed a set of 15-30-30 in 115-145-135 msec with 15/0 ratio, respectively. During this session we also used other psychological techniques, such as relaxation (10-15 min), relaxation while listening to music (10-15 min), and concentration exercise with biofeedback (5-10 min). The judoka felt ready for his crucial

60

competition; he reported that he was satisfied with his psychological readiness. It should be mentioned that a day or so before the competition the athlete's perceived stress increased. The sport psychologist spent some time with the judoka on the night before the fight and provided him with a "last minute" psychological session. The final standing of this judoka was fifth place.

Similar protocols were used with both male and female elite athletes in preparation for the 2004 Olympic Games. On one instance during these games, a day before a judo competition, the same judoka performed a set of 15-30-30 in 107-136-117 msec, respectively, and was awarded the bronze medal on the following day. Thus, these protocols may be individualized for use with each elite combat athlete tailored to his/her seasonal goals, athletic achievements, motivational level, and individual personality.

Moreover, RT programs integrate with other psychological strategies and link with preparation phases (see examples 1 and 2).

Example 1. Mental training session in GP (Judo)

Task: Improve concentration, psychomotor abilities.

Techniques: RTP, concentration exercises, biofeedback training.

Place: Lab setting (11-11:50), November, 2006.

1. RTP – Set of 15-30-30 RTs performed with a time limit of 175-185-170 msec with 7/8 or 8/7 ratios, 5 times.

2. Concentration exercises with GSR biofeedback control 15 times X 5 sec, 10 times X10 sec.

3. Relaxation with GSR_{BFB} – 10 min (GSR – galvanic skin response; BFB – biofeedback).

Example 2. Mental training session in SP (Judo)

Task: Developing competition strategies.

Techniques: RTP with stress factors, imagery, relaxation.

Place: Lab setting (13:00-14:00), April, 2005.

1. RTP with competition noises. Set of 15-30-30 RTs with time limit 155-165-160 msec, 11/4 ratio, 3 times; set of 10-20-20 RTs with time limit 155-165-155 msec 8/2 ratio, 3 times.

2. Imagery judo match Israel-Holland with GSR control and competition noises – 5 min with next relaxation 5 min (see Figure 3.4).

3. Biofeedback games – 10 min.

Figure 3.4. PST session protocol in judo.

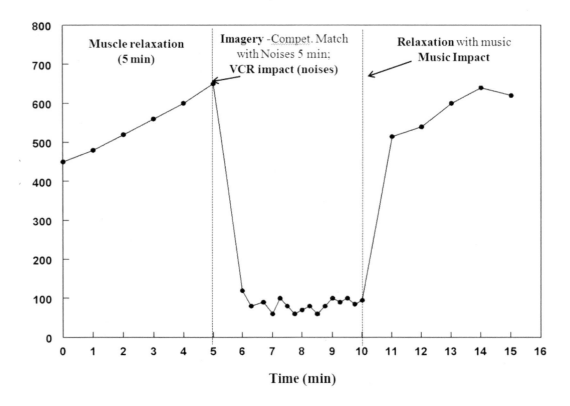

In this session the aim was to demonstrate how psychological preparation is integrated with other training preparations, such as the physical, technical, and tactical, within the three critical phases of the training program. The response training program was selected to exhibit the applied procedures that should be used during the different training phases. Other psychological techniques, such as imagery and relaxation, can be developed and applied in the same manner. In our view, the practitioner must integrate the psychological preparation into these components within each of the three phases. If this is done, the psychological component is naturally synthesized into the "theory of training."

Taekwondo – one of the two martial arts (together with judo) that was included in the Olympic Games as medal-winning events. This self-defense sport includes "both physical technique and the performer's mental and spiritual association with these techniques. It's a discipline of both mind and body" (Anshel & Payne, 2006, p. 355). Taekwondo is based on foot techniques (i.e., short, quick, powerful strikes and chops). Among the psychological skills required in taekwondo (as in judo) are self-regulation, concentration, confidence, self-talking, and anticipation (Blumenstein et al., 2005). Competitive fights in Taekwondo last 3 rounds, 2 min each, with 1-min pauses between rounds. PST programs for taekwondo include many specific points, but the main goal is "to achieve a state of mind in which the performer is acutely aware of the endlessly changing competition environment and can effortlessly react to such changes" (Park & Seabourne, 1997, p. 14).

The most popular cognitive strategies that we applied in taekwondo were:

- ❖ Reaction Training Program (RTP)
- ❖ Fast concentration during 10, 20 sec with GSR and EMG control
- ❖ Muscle relaxation with EMG control
- ❖ Imagery of the competition fights again specific athletes
- ❖ Relaxation with music and biofeedback
- ❖ Self-talking and positive thinking in the competition routine
- ❖ Biofeedback training.

One of the mental sessions in the competition period is presented in the following example.

Example 3. Mental training session in competition period (taekwondo).

Task: developing competition strategies.

Techniques: RTP with stress factors, imagery competition fight, relaxation

Place: Lab setting (before main training 9-10.00), September, 2007

1. Concentration exercises with GSR 10 times X30 sec (Δ GSR $\approx$ 5-10kΩ indicates an good physiological response)

2. RTP with competition noises set of 5-10-10 RTs with a time limit of 165-175-160μsec X 3 times with 1 min pause between sets.

3. Imagery taekwondo fight Israel-Germany 3 X 2 min with GSR control and competition noises, then 5 min relaxation pause (Figure 3.5).

4. Muscle relaxation – 10 min.

Figure 3.5. PST session example protocol in taekwondo. Imagery competition match duration is 3X2 min.

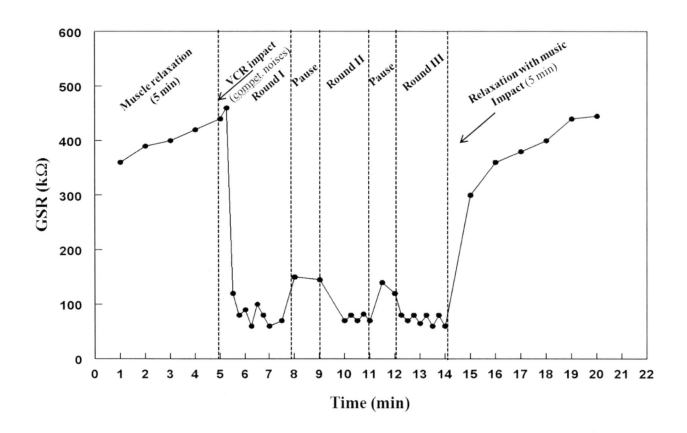

Track and Field – Pole Vault. During competition, athletes are allowed three attempts to clear a previously chosen height. Decisions regarding the height they choose to jump can prove crucial in achieving victory. There are rather long pauses between attempts, and the athlete must organize his/her behavior during this time period. Pole vault demands a high level of physical and technical preparation. Some of the important psychological skills include: concentration, self-regulation (relaxation-excitation waves), imagery, thought control, and self-confidence.

One of the strategies applied in our work was biofeedback (BFB) training (Blumenstein, Bar-Eli, Collins, 2002); and among the different BFB exercises, the more popular were:

- ❖ Fast concentration during 10, 20 sec with GSR_{BFB} control (good result for this exercise is $\Delta GSR \approx 20\text{-}30k\Omega$)

- ❖ Fast concentration during 10, 20 sec with positive (M^+), negative (M^-) verbal impact with GSR control

- ❖ Fast concentration during 30 sec with GSR_{BFB} control (good result for this exercise is $\Delta GSR \approx 30\text{-}50k\Omega$)

- ❖ Muscle relaxation – excitation waves with GSR_{BFB} (EMG from baseline to 0.8-1.0 µv and from 0.8-1.0 µv to 2.2-2.4 µv during 2-3 min)

- ❖ Imagery of the competition jumps with EMG and GSR control. All processes were measured with a stopper.

- ❖ Imagery of the competition behavior; develop precompetition routine.

- ❖ Relaxation (10 min), then imagery precompetition routine, then jump (i.e., 5.65) and relaxation 5 min, etc.

Integration of these exercises in the training process is presented in Table 3.3.

Table 3.3. An example of the integration of all psychological techniques applied during the pole vault training process

Phase	Psychological exercises	Treatment mode and duration (session X time)	Comments
Preparation	Concentration exercise with GSR BFB	25-30 X 20-30 sec	Lab setting
	Relaxation with EMG BFB	10-15 X 10-20 min	
	Imagery with GSR BFB	25-30 X 5-10 min	
	BFB games	10-15 X 5-10 min	Lab-Training setting
	Pre-competition routine	10-15 X 3-5 min	
Competition	Rapid concentration exercises with GSR BFB	25-30 X 10-20 sec	Lab setting
	Rapid concentration with GSR BFB and M^+, M^-	25-30 X 10-20 sec	
	Relaxation– excitation waves with EMG/GSR BFB	25-30 X 2-3 min	Lab-Training setting
	Competition jumps imagery (technical side)	40-50 X1-2 min	
	Imagery: Pre-jump routine and jump	20-30 X3-2 min	Lab setting
	Relaxation with GSR/ EMG BFB	10-15 X 10-15 min	
Transition	Relaxation with EMG/GSR BFB	3-5 X 15-20 min	Lab setting
	Concentration exercise	5-10 X 5-10 sec	

Where M+ and M- = positive and negative motivation, respectively; lab=laboratory

Rhythmic Gymnastics (Individual and Team)

In the preparation phase, a "map of difficulties" is developed together with the gymnast and her coach, for each gymnast. In this map all the difficult places (critical positions) in the gymnast's exercise are marked. Each combination (ball, clubs, hoop, ribbon, and rope) has its own map of difficulties.

For example, the gymnast wrote 19 key words which marked the critical positions in her ball combination (see Figure 3.6):

Figure 3.6. "Map of difficulties" for ball combination in rhythmic gymnastics (before mental training)

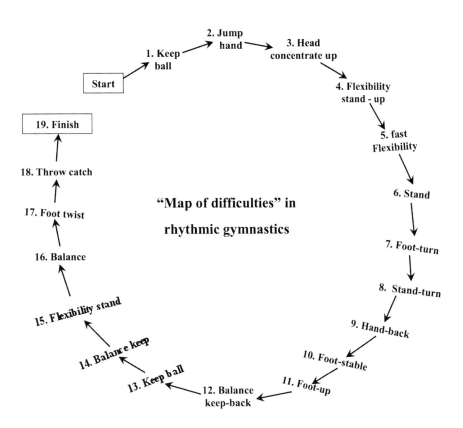

Start: 1. Keep ball → 2. Jump-hand → 3. Head-concentrate up → 4. Flexibility – stand-up → Fast flexibility → 6. Stand → 7. Foot-turn → 8. Stand-turn → 9. Hand-back →10. Foot-stable → 11. Foot-up → 12. Balance – keep back → 13. Keep ball → 14. Balance keep → 15. Flexibility – stand → 16. Balance → 17. Foot-twist → 18. Throw-catch → 19. Finish.

In order to understand these critical positions and the coaches' remarks, recommendations and demands, we were present at many training sessions, during which these ball combinations (and others) were used. In the laboratory setting the gymnasts images these ball combinations and tries to perform them accurately and correctly. At the beginning imagery and at the end, the gymnast gave a signal with her finger, at which point the time for this combination was accurately measured (combination must last 1.30 sec).

In the beginning this imagery combination lasted 2.10-2.15 min, but we tried to have the gymnast perform all the combinations accurately and correctly; this was my main purpose. After one month of mental training (10-12 mental sessions), a 1.45-1.46 sec imagery performance was achieved by the gymnast. We made a new "map of difficulties," and this time it had only 8 critical positions. It should be noted that we changed the context of these critical positions from describing only the movements in the first map to describing the emotional and mental state in the second map (e.g., smile, concentrate, confidence; see Figure 3.7).

Figure 3.7. "Map of difficulties" for ball combination in rhythmic gymnastics (following mental training)

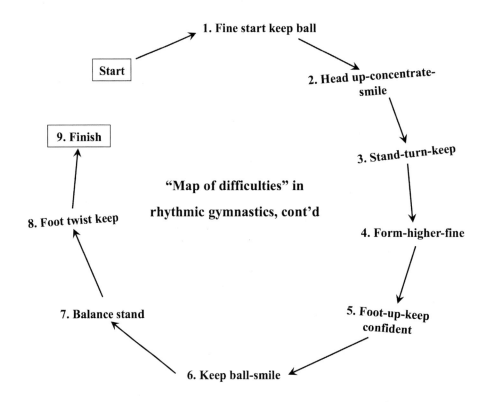

Start: 1. Fine start – keep ball → 2. Head up – concentrate – smile → 3. Stand-turn-keep → 4.

Form – higher – fine → 5. Foot up – keep – confident → 6. Keep ball - smile → 7. Balance – stand

→ 8. Foot-twist-keep → Finish.

After about 10 mental sessions we achieved 1.30-1.35 sec in imagery performance, and improved

not only the gymnast's performance but also the coach's and gymnast's mood, and the cooperation

between them in training. Before competition only 3 critical positions with emotional context were

in our map.

For team rhythmic gymnastics (5 persons), the same principles and PST program were applied. In

the preparation phase a "map of group difficulties" was developed together with coaches and

gymnasts. Moreover, we attended several training sessions in order to understand these critical

positions and the coach's remarks and demands during the gymnastic performance.

Two main interventional programs were used in the individual and group meetings: The Wingate

Five-Step Approach (W5-SA) (Blumenstein, Bar-Eli, Tenenbaum, 2002), and a specific

psychological training program (Blumenstein & Lidor, 2008), which was composed of mental skills

techniques, such as focusing attention, relaxation, self-talk, imagery individual and group), that were

developed by the first author throughout many years of professional practice.

These techniques have also been used by many sport psychology consultants who work with elite

athletes (e.g., Henschen, 2005; Kremer & Moran, 2008; Moran, 2005). However, several main

points need to be explained.

The individual meetings took place in the psychological laboratory. The main objective of these

meetings was to enable the gymnasts to practice the interventional techniques, to help them to be

mentally prepared for practice and competitions, and for us to obtain good psychological contact

with each gymnast.

After about 10 laboratory mental sessions (2 times per week, each session lasting 45-50 min), we achieved good individual imagery performance in the time limit between 2:33 (min:sec) to 2:35 with each gymnast (combinations must last 2:30).

Then we continued with group meetings, mainly they took part after practice in the gymnastic hall. The first group's imagery performance was very disordered. The gymnasts were instructed to close their eyes and, when a signal was given, to imagine one of their group exercises. When each of them finished the exercise, they signaled with their hand and the time was recorded. The first finished after 2:16 (min:sec), the second – 2:47, the third at 2:50, fourth and fifth 2:57.

After 7-8 group meetings, we achieved optimal results in limit 2 min 29 sec – 2 min 32 sec. Coaches noted better group performance in practice, and the gymnasts were concentrated better and were more confident during their performance. Although during the mental sessions all the gymnasts significantly improved their relaxation and self-talk skills, there was a general rise in group self-confidence. These positive changes were felt in several competitions, and especially during the Beijing Olympic Games in 2008. The gymnasts perform excellent combinations in the competitions and achieved sixth place. These examples with rhythmic gymnastics illustrate the link between the real training process and PST.

Team Sports. Two instances of PST in team sports are hereby described, one in soccer and the other in basketball. In both cases the coaches initiated our psychological intervention with their teams. We worked with two soccer teams from the National League (Division 1) and provided psychological services to the national basketball teams in several seasons from 2000-2004 (cadet, youth, separate for girls/boys). From this experience we developed a special approach to PST in team sports (Blumenstein et al., 2007; Lidor, Blumenstein, & Tenenbaum, 2007), which includes:

1. PST on a daily basis in the laboratory or in a room in the local team's stadium/hall.

2. PST in training camp (from 21 days abroad until 2-3 months before European Championship in basketball).

3. PST on a systematic basis with 2-3 perspective young basketball players (10 months – 1 season) or 2-3 problematic soccer players who needed our support.

4. Weekly (or daily in basketball) meetings with the coaching staff, and developing our recommendations for the game, especially in soccer.

Among the more popular techniques and strategies in team sports were biofeedback training, concentration exercises, self-talk, and relaxation. During the preparation phase we held individual sessions, with the goal of improving the player's concentration, muscle relaxation, positive thinking, etc. We discussed pre-game routines, players' self-confidence, and motivation. Players reacted positively to these meetings, especially in training camp, and were often curious to know "Who is best?" in this or another mental exercise. During our meetings they received a great deal of psychological information on mental preparation for the game, and received various recommendations for concrete game situations. These situations may include correcting mistakes, resuming their concentration; concentration with self-talk; learning how to reduce emotional arousal before a game; player behavior the day before a game, etc.

During the competition phase, soccer teams played one game per week; they practiced every day and we were present during the weekly game. We provided psychological services during numerous meetings, per the request of the coach (especially before the game), and worked with many young players who were playing for the first time in the season, as well as with players who were asked to play a different position than the one they were used to. The main objective of these meetings was to enhance self-confidence, concentration, and positive thinking (see Dosil, 2006; Lidor et al., 2007).

During the competition phase, individual and team/small group mental sessions were provided. The objective of these meetings for the basketball team was to assist some of the players in coping with mental barriers, such as lack of motivation after losing games and lack of playing time in game, and to improve cooperation with players and pre-competitive scheduled routines. For that purpose, we used imagery and self-talk techniques to assist players in developing game plans and memorizing offensive and defensive team maneuvers, and in developing pre-free-throw shot routines for each player.

In addition, we focused on team cohesion and conducted a few group dynamic sessions, in order to build leadership as well as to foster a positive climate among the team members (Henschen & Cook, 2005; Lidor et al., 2007). It should be noted the there is a high number of foreign soccer and basketball players in elite clubs. Therefore, in our work we had to consider cultural differences such as language barriers, ethnic standards, music preferences and cultural-based understanding of discipline (Lidor & Blumenstein, 2009).

PST before Main Competition

The first author (BB) served as a sport psychology consultant for the 1996, 2000, 2004, and 2008 Israeli Olympic teams, and took part in Olympic preparation in the former USSR teams (1984, 1988). In this section we will present general recommendations and reflections on PST before major events, including the Olympic Games. It is clear that PST was provided for the athletes and their coaches not only during the Olympic Games (World or European Championships), but throughout the 4 years that preceded the Games. During this precompetition period PST was usually applied to improve three areas: concentration, confidence, composure or self-regulation.

The following represent the most popular psychological techniques that we used:

For concentration –

- Biofeedback training (Blumenstein, Bar-Eli, Collins, 2002)

- Pre-performance routines (Lidor & Singer, 2003; Moran, 1996) or pre-competition routines (Henschen, 2005)

- Self-talk (Gould, Eklund, & Jackson, 1993)

- Breathing exercises (Moran, 1996; Williams & Harris, 2001)

- RTP (Blumenstein et al., 2005).

For confidence –

- Biofeedback training (Blumenstein, Bar-Eli, Collins, 2002)

- RTP (Blumenstein et al., 2005)

- Positive self-talk (Gould et al., 1993; Moran, 1996)

- Pre-performance mental routines (Lidor & Singer, 2003; Moran, 1996) or pre-competition routines (Henschen, 2005)

- Imagery (Blumenstein et al., 2007).

For composure –

- Relaxation with biofeedback (Blumenstein, Bar-Eli, Collins, 2002)

- Arousal regulation (Weinberg & Williams, 2001; Williams & Harris, 2001)

- Attention control (Nideffer, 1989).

PST before/during the competition setting was provided in four phases (for the Olympic Games): Habituation, Psychological Routine, Specific Psychological Preparation, and Recovery (Table 3.4).

Table 3.4. Psychological preparation for main competition – Olympic Games (the 4-Phase approach)

Phase	Duration (days)		Objective(s)	Framework(s)
	Short-term, Barcelona, 1992; Athens, 2004	Long-term, Sydney, 2000; Beijing, 2008		
1. Habituation	2	3	Overcome jetlag, adopt to the Village atmosphere, organization of the PST	Individual and Group sessions
2. Psychological routine	2	6-10	PST routines	Individual session Group session (in training)
3. Specific Psychological Preparation	2-4	2-4	Specific preparation for the competitive event	Individual sessions (in room and training settings)
4. Recovery	1-2	1-2	Recovery from physical /psychological effort exerted during the main competitions in the Olympic Games	Individual session (room)

This approach was described in detail by Blumenstein and Lidor (2008). It should be noted that this example presents PST for short to long periods (e.g. 1-3 weeks) before the Olympic Games. Naturally, one understands that Table 3.4 cannot include every circumstance; therefore decisions were often taken instantaneously according to concrete situations, based on our experience, coach-athlete relationships, and numerous other factors.

To summarize, we hope that in this chapter we were successful in clarifying that:

❖ PST is an integrative approach to developing athletes' mental skills, like other training preparations, and is part of the general training process.

❖ PST is critical for athletic success, especially in major competitive events.

❖ PST is a long, systematic process with its own techniques and strategies, planning, and periodizations.

❖ PST is individual and specific for each kind of sport.

In this chapter we have discussed numerous general and specific examples relating to PST and performance enhancement. However, a number of common problems have been identified by athletes, coaches, and sport psychologists/consultants:

a) Lack of time for PST

b) Most coaches are not ready for systematic and long-term PST

c) Coaches' lack of knowledge about PST

d) Coaches and athletes expect immediate results/effects following 2-3 weeks of PST

e) Consultants' lack of knowledge about sport training

f) Lack of full cooperation between coach-athlete-consultant

g) Coach and athlete often blame the consultant's work for any failures.

We hope that this chapter will help athletes and coaches better understand the potential of PST. The next chapter will focus on the relationships that the sport psychology consultant establishes during the training process, and the ethical foundations of his/her psychological services.

References

Anshel, M., & Payne, M. (2006). Application of sport psychology for optimal performance in martial arts. In J. Dosil (Ed.), *The sport psychologist's handbook: A guide for sport-specific performance enhancement* (pp. 353-374). Chichester, UK: Wiley.

Blumenstein, B., & Lidor, R. (2008). Psychological preparations in the Olympic Village. *International Journal of Sport and Exercise Psychology, 3,* 287-300.

Blumenstein, B., Bar-Eli, M., & Collins, D. (2002). Biofeedback training in sport. In B. Blumenstein, M. Bar-Eli, & G. Tenenbaum. *Brain and body in sport and exercise: Biofeedback applications in performance enhancement* (pp. 55-76). Chichester, UK: Wiley.

Blumenstein, B., Bar-Eli, M., & Tenenbaum, G. (2002). (Eds.). *Brain and body in sport and exercise: Biofeedback applications in performance enhancement.* Chichester, UK: Wiley.

Blumenstein, B., Lidor, R., & Tenenbaum, G. (2005). Periodization and planning of psychological preparation in elite combat sport programs: The case of judo. *International Journal of Sport and Exercise Psychology, 3,* 7-25.

Blumenstein, B., Lidor, R., & Tenenbaum, G. (2007). (Eds.), *Psychology of sport training.* Oxford, UK: Meyer and Meyer Sport.

Blumenstein, B., & Orbach, I. Biofeedback training in Sea. In A. Edmonds & G. Tenenbaum (Eds). *Case studies in applied psychophysiology: Neurofeedback and biofeedback treatment for advances in human performance. Wiley-Blackwell,* In Press.

Dosil, J. (2006). (Ed.). *The sport psychologist's handbook: A guide for sport-specific performance enhancement.* Chichester, UK: Wiley.

Duran-Bush, N., & Salmela, J. (2002). The development and maintenance of expert athletic performance: Perceptions of world and Olympic champions. *Journal of Applied Sport Psychology, 14,* 154-171.

Gould, D., & Carson, S. (2007). Psychological preparation in sport. In B. Blumenstein, R. Lidor, & G. Tenenbaum (Eds.), *Psychology of sport training* (pp. 115-136). Oxford, UK: Meyer and Meyer Sport.

Gould, D., & Damarjian, N. (1998). Mental skills training in sport. In B. Elliot (Ed.), *Applied sport science: Training in sport. International Handbook of Sport Science* (Vol. 3, pp. 69-116). Sussex, England: Wiley.

Gould, D., Eklund, R., & Jackson, S. (1993). Coping strategies used by U.S. Olympic wrestlers. *Research Quarterly for Exercise and Sport, 64,* 83-93.

Greenspan, M., & Feltz, D. (1989). Psychological interventions with athletes in competitive situations: A review. *The Sport Psychologist, 3,* 219-236.

Henschen, K. (2005). Mental practice – skill oriented. In D. Hackfort, J. Duda, & R. Lidor (Eds.), *Handbook of research in applied sport and exercise psychology: International perspectives* (pp. 19-34). Morgantown, WV: Fitness Informational Technology.

Henschen, K., & Cook, D. (2005). Working with professional basketball players. In R. Lidor & K. Henschen (Eds.), *The psychology of team sports* (pp. 143-160). Morgantown, WV: Fitness Information Technology.

Jacobson, E. (1930). *Progressive relaxation.* Chicago: University of Chicago Press.

Kremer, J., & Moran, A. (2008). Pure Sport: Practical Sport Pyschology, Routledge: Taylor & Francis Group, London and NY.

Lidor, R., Blumenstein, B., & Tenenbaum, G. (2007). Periodization and planning of psychological preparation in individual and team sports. In: B. Blumenstein, R. Lidor, G. Tenenbaum (Eds.), *Psychology of Sport Training* (pp. 137-161). Oxford, UK: Meyer & Meyer Sports.

Lidor, R., Blumenstein, B. (2009). Working with elite athletes in Israel In R. Schinke & S. Hanrahan (Eds.). *Cultural Sport Psychology* (pp. 141-152). Champaign, IL, Human Kinetics.

Lidor, R., & Singer, R. (2003). Preperformance routines in self-paced tasks: Development and educational considerations. In R. Lidor & K. Henschen (Eds.), *The psychology of team sports* (pp. 69-98). Morgantown, WV: Fitness Information Technology.

Martens, R., Vealey, R., & Burton, D. (1990). *Competitive anxiety in sport*. Champaign, IL: Human Kinetics.

Moran, A. (1996). *The psychology of concentration in sport performers: A cognitive analysis.* Hove, East Sussex: Psychology Press.

Moran, A. (2005). Training attention and concentration skills in athletes. In D. Hackfort, J. Duda, & R. Lidor (Eds.), *Handbook of research in applied sport and exercise psychology: International perspectives* (pp. 61-74). Morgantown, WV: Fitness Information Technology.

Morris, R., & Thomas, P. (1995). Approaches to applied sport psychology. In T. Morris & J. Summers (Eds.), *Sport psychology: Theory, application and issues* (pp. 215-258). Singapore: Weley.

Nideffer, R. (1989). *Attention control training for sport.* San Diego, CA: Educational and Industrial Testing Service.

Orlick, T. (1986). *Psyching for sport: Mental training for athletes.* Champaign, IL: Human Kinetics.

Park, Y., & Seabourne, T. (1997). *Taekwondo techniques and tactics*. Champaign, IL: Human Kinetics.

Pedro, J., & Durbin, W. (2001). *Judo: Techniques and tactics.* Champaign, IL: Human Kinetics.

Singer, R. (1988). Strategies and metastrategies in learning and performing self-paced athletic skills. *Sport Psychologist, 2,* 49-68.

Spielberger, C, Gorsuch, R & Luchene, R. (1970). *Manual for the state-trait anxiety inventory.* Palo Alto, CA. Consulting Psychological Press.

Suinn, R. (1993). Imagery. In R. Singer, M. Murphey, & L. Tennant (Eds.), *Handbook of research on sport psychology* (p. 492-510). New York: Macmillan.

Vealey, R. (1994). Current status and prominent issues in sport psychology interventions. *Medicine and Science in Sports and Exercise, 26,* 495-502.

Vealey, R. (1998). Future directions in psychological skills training. *Sport Psychologist, 2,* 318-336.

Vealey, R. (2005). *Coaching for the inner edge.* Morgantown, WV: Fitness Information Technology.

Vealey, R. (2007). Mental skills training in sport. In G. Tenenbaum & R. Eklund (Eds.), *Handbook of sport psychology* (3rd ed., pp. 287-309). New York: Wiley.

Weinberg, R., & Williams, J. (2001). Integrating and implementing a psychological skills training program. In J. Williams (Ed.), *Applied sport psychology: Personal growth to peak performance* (4th ed., pp. 347-377). Mountain View, CA: Mayfield.

Williams, J., & Harris, D. (2001). Relaxation and energizing techniques for regulation of arousal. In J. Williams (Ed.), *Applied sport psychology: Personal growth to peak performance* (4th ed., pp. 229-246). Mountain View: Mayfield.

Chapter 4. The Sport Psychology Consultant

Applied sport psychology is a fairly young profession, developed in the former USSR during the 1950s (Garfield & Bennett, 1984) and in the West during the 1970s (Vealey, 2007; Weinberg & Williams, 2001).

What is a sport psychology consultant, and what are the main functions and roles fulfilled by the consultant? These are a few of the questions which will be discussed in this chapter. Many athletes (especially younger ones) feel that if they consult with a sport psychologist, then something must be psychologically wrong or problematical with them. However, if an athlete wishes to consult with the fitness coach or his/her personal coach on a particular move or physical technique, the athlete is applauded for making an extra effort to improve. Weinberg and Williams (2001) noted that the same attitude must be applied to both of these instances: "If an athlete realizes that he or she needs to work on some aspect of the mental game, such as concentration skills, then this also should be applauded" (p. 357). However, why is this not happening today? We think that both coaches and athletes do not fully understand the possibilities of psychological skills training (PST); they do not know the precise way in which PST contributes to athlete ability, and therefore do not comprehend most of the positive changes (improvements) that can be brought about by PST. Moreover, coaches and athletes do not comprehend that PST, with great potential for performance enhancement, should actually be part of the training process. Furthermore, establishment of good relationship between the coaches and the sport psychology consultants from the beginning of the process is a key for a fruitful PST program, eventually resulting in athletic performance improvement.

Sport psychology consultants should be close to sport in order to understand sport from within, through trainings and competitions, and they must understand and absorb the unique sport atmosphere of training and competition stress (Cox, 2007; Henschen, 2005; Ravizza, 2001).

Moreover, we (sport psychologists/consultants/ mental coaches) must also understand who we are – are we helpers? coaches? referees? experts? initiators?

Cooperation with the Coaches and Athletes

In this chapter we wish to describe some practical situations of working with athletes and coaches. We will discuss the first author's (referred to as BB) educational approach, some critical lessons that we have learned, and ethical considerations in sport psychology consultations.

In the following examples of consultations, we will attempt to demonstrate the above considerations in some practical situations, and we will discuss and explain our place in the "coach-athlete" infrastructure.

Educational approach in consulting. Our approach focuses on mental aspects of performance enhancement which, like physical training, consist of educational processes. Founded on BB's 35 years of experience in this field, we firmly believe that mental skills can be developed, just like physical skills.

The main points of this approach include:

1. Transfer psychological (theoretical, research-based) information to the coach and athlete (or team);

2. Develop sport-specific mental skills;

3. Support the integration of the athlete's mental skills in practice and competition.

Transfer psychological information for coach and athlete. The coach and the athlete have neither the time nor the possibility to search for modern psychological information or research recommendations in the area of sport psychology. However, the sport psychologist has excellent opportunities to present relevant psychological information to the coach and the athlete, and to establish a good relationship with them both. Naturally, the information provided must be important and relevant to the training process and to performance enhancement. Moreover, this information must be understandable to the coach and the athlete; the failure of the sport psychology consultant to understand sport and athletic performance will hinder his/her cooperation with the coach and athlete, and can ultimately end their professional relationships (Blumenstein, 2001).

From the first meeting, the sport psychology consultant is expected to listen carefully to the coach and the athlete and learn what they are currently doing, listen to their problems, and hear what their expectations are from cooperating with the consultant. Moreover, the consultant will provide a possible framework and a schedule of future cooperation in these initial meetings.

Developing relevant mental skills. We usually begin with performance-enhancement skills and teach athletes self-regulation skills, such as relaxation techniques, imagery, and biofeedback training. This process consists of three stages. The athletes go through 1) the **basic learning** stage under laboratory settings (acquire techniques); 2) the **distractions** stage in a laboratory setting (performing these techniques with various distractions (see Chapter 3); and 3) the **application** stage (performing these techniques at daily practices and during competitions).

During the next stage, we teach the athletes to concentrate with pre-performance routines, self-talking, and biofeedback training. Again, they go through the same three stages (learning, distractions, application).

Mental skills should be related to performance, and thus concentration and relaxation in shooting (concentrate on the target) is not the same as in tennis (concentrate on the ball and the opponent); rhythmic gymnastic self-regulation (balanced) is not the same as in basketball or soccer (higher level and dynamic).

We developed mental skills programs for the athletes which is directly related to performance and to the athletes as individuals (see Blumenstein & Bar-Eli, 2001; Blumenstein & Lidor, 2004; Blumenstein, Lidor, & Tenenbaum, 2005).

<u>Supporting the integration of mental skills during practice and competition</u>. The final part of our educational approach is to support the integration of mental skills during practice, and to transfer skills from the laboratory to the field. This is a critical issue, since we are judged by the athlete and coaches according to their achievements during competition. The sport psychologist consultant should attend athletes' practices and competitions, and provide recommendations and comments to the athletes and coaches; often the mere presences of the consultant may serve as a "reminder" or a "trigger" for the athletes to make use of their mental plan.

We often help the athletes apply their mental skills in specific situations before competitions (before and after warm-up), such as between attempts in the pole vault, between races in canoeing/kayaking or windsurfing, between matches in judo or taekwondo, between quarters or before replacement in basketball, and during breaks in the action of games such as tennis and basketball.

We will attempt to describe several cases using BB's experience. Presenting some practical situations will help us discuss and enable the understanding of our role in the "coach-athlete" system.

Case 1. Ideal Variant (A$^+$, C$^+$)

Both the coach (C) and athlete (A) wish to use the sport psychology consultant services in their team to improve some athlete's psychological skills and to prepare for several competitions (over a long-term period).

Our role in this case is very effective, as we are a member of a team, but only as a <u>helper</u>. This is an important point for the sport psychology consultant, as we are not the head coach, but rather are experts in the field of psychology. We provide recommendations to the coach according to the athlete's psychological preparations and work on improving his or her psychological skills, just like any other preparation (see Chapter 1). We participate in training practices and competitions, strengthen the "coach-athlete" relationship, and teach the coach and athlete how to cope with training and competition stress. There were situations in which BB was considered as a referee for solving disagreements. But it should be stressed that our main role is to be a helper and a mental coach. An example is presented below.

Soccer player M was one of the best players in the soccer team, a senior player (5 years with a dominant role in the team). His success began when he was young, therefore he was invited to play in the junior and adult national teams. In these teams he was always a leader and consistently played a dominant role. He liked to get respect from the other players ("I'm the best, I'm a goal maker, I make the points"), but he did not always give respect to others. He was very careful with the coaching staff, but if he made many mistakes in a match he would blame the other players ("I don't get good balls; I run and am not good situation; the other players don't help me…"). He was not friendly with the other members of the team, and had only one (foreign) friend on the team; he only socialized during practice or official meetings with other players. BB had worked for this team since the beginning of the season as a consultant to the new coaching staff, to some players, and occasionally to the club managers. BB usually met with the team (players) once or twice a week (before or after a match) according to the head coach's request, and once a month with the team's professional staff (coaches, medical, team officials).

The coaches called BB every day in the beginning. While discussing BB's work with the head coach and manager, the coach asked BB to take on M as a special project in the team ("help him improve his communicative ability with other players, and to improve his self-regulation, especially during a match; he does not feel he is part of the team, he feels he only "works" for the team, …). BB decided to act in two directions: begin with changing/improving the team position (other players) toward M, as well as M's own vision towards his teammates, not only during training but also off training and competitions.

BB invited the players for the weekly meetings (before or after practice, or in the hotel when they were all together (pre-season training camps, in-season breaks, etc.). BB began working with M., discussing his strong technical and physical characteristics, and less his tactical and mental ones. BB proposed that M improve the psychological skills – self-regulation, concentration, and self-talking – that would improve his general skills as a player. Later we only talked about his psychological skills, in meetings 1-2 times per week before training, each session lasting 30-40 min.

After several weeks, during which M participated in all the meetings on a regular basis, we observed progress in M's psycho-regulation (by use of BFB techniques, relaxation, imagery, and self-talking techniques). M preferred exercises with BFB equipment, because he understood what he must do, think, and say when he wanted to concentrate, relax, correct his mistakes, or correct his behavior. During our meetings we discussed several topics, including his future place in the team, his views on the positive and negative aspects of the team, his relations with players and others. BB understood M's apprehensions ("I must save and defend my position in the team") and delusions ("they do not like me", or "the new coach doesn't know me and I'm afraid to make mistakes").

Together with the officials and coaching staff, we organized four informal free-evening meetings with all the players, in order to establish better cohesion and friendship among the team members (on one occasion with their spouses and friends). Paying attention to the ethnic variability of team, various ethnic foods were served. We decided not to focus on national or cultural individuality during these meetings, as but considered these in our daily work (holidays, language, traditions). We were very attentive to the players' requests, such as food, fasting habits, religious holidays, etc., and demanded the same of the players (especially foreign ones). After two months, the coach and the player himself noted a significant improvement in M's performance, as he scored three goals in the last two games, and there was a positive change in his ranking among team players. This case illustrates successful cooperation and a successful outcome.

Case 2 (A⁺, C⁻)

Sometimes the athlete wishes to use the services of a sport psychology consultant, but the coach is skeptical or does not agree. BB began from a conflict situation and had to work very carefully with the athlete, because the coach was looking for "reasons" to justify his initial negative attitude. The consultant was cautioned against trying to turn the athlete against the coach or "replacing" the coach's position.

A striking example occurred when BB was working with elite Soviet track and field athletes in accordance with the Soviet Sport Committee "recommendations." The athletes were happy to meet with BB (a new feature in the usually monotonous practice), however the head coach was rather skeptical (perhaps he was ill-informed about the role of a sport psychology consultant), but he accepted this decision; he was not helpful but did not upset the situation either. After 2-3 months of joint work, the head coach asked BB to make a prognosis before a USA-USSR traditional track and field competition, to predict which of the Soviet athletes would perform well in this competition, and who would be the most mentally prepared. BB prepared a list of a dozen athletes; the coach placed it in a box without even looking, and said "after the competition we will discuss your prognosis."

Needless to say, BB was very worried throughout the competition, perhaps even more than the athletes were. After the competition we discussed the athletes' results (an unusual coach-staff meeting), and at the end of the meeting the coach said that his sport psychology consultant helped his athletes and that he knows track and field; 10 (out of 12) of BB's prognoses were correct. After this competition, the coach assisted BB in various training situations and became very interested in sport psychology, with many of his observations and considerations being quite important to BB.

In this case BB was the initiator, expert and helper, however, he realized that the results could have been be strikingly different, with a sad ending – that is, if the athletes did not win, this unusual meeting would have been the last one for BB in this sport event.

87

However, we must be very assertive in the choice of possibilities, and special attention must be given to the relationship with coaches.

Case 3 (A⁻, C⁺)

The coach invited a sport psychology consultant to help his/her athlete; the athlete was skeptical or even against this move, but agreed to participate in 1-2 meetings. This was a unique situation in which one must explain and demonstrate to the athlete his/her difficulties and ways to overcome this barrier. BB used biofeedback techniques and other accurate indicators to point-out the athlete's actual psychological skills' development under different stress situations. Additionally, there was a need to review what occurred during competitions and to provide recommendations to the athlete (about time period, approximate total number of meetings, when he/she will see changes, etc.).

The athletes were fascinated with this approach; BB presented them with a concrete plan and the athletes understood, as they were able to observe their progress during each session. After 1-1½ months the athletes attempted to apply many of the mental training elements to their practice. Here the sports psychology consultant served as the initiator, helper, and the expert.

These three cases demonstrate that we are first of all sport psychology consultants, helpers, and mental coaches, but in many instances we must also serve as referees, initiators, and researchers. This is true because each new athletes or new team stimulates a new, challenging project of exploration. If an athlete and a coach win, we obtain positive research results, and if they lose, we have bad results. Real-life situations are more complex than those described in these three cases; relationships and cooperation between athlete-coach-sport psychologists are multifaceted, as will be presented below.

Psychological consultants must be ready to provide traditional mental sessions in laboratory settings, and also be prepared to visit athletes in training and accompany athletes and coaches to numerous competitions, and help them with different living and competition situations.

The following three cases will demonstrate a number of these real-life situations.

Case 1 – Judo. Before the competition (European Judo Championships) BB worked with an athlete for one year. After three winning fights that took place in one morning, the judoka reported to the coach: "I don't have energy and I want to sleep." The coach replied: "What, you have 30-35 min until the next match, go to warm-up, increase your motivation level, and if you win we will watch the finals on TV later on…" BB talked with the coach and proposed that the athlete rest for 20-25 min. "I will make sure sleeps, and then he will do a short warm-up, and he will be revitalized before the match. The coach agreed and passed on full responsibility to BB, saying "I don't have time", "I must go with the other athletes to the match". We allocated a quiet place for the judoka, and he immediately fell asleep. After 20 min BB woke him up and he commenced a short warm-up. In short, the judoka won "yuko" during the first two minutes, during the subsequent 3 min both judokas were rather fatigued and were penalized for a passive match, but those first 2 minutes awarded victory and a medal to our judoka.

Case 2 – Windsurfing. Before the world windsurfing championship, BB worked with a windsurfer for about one year. Two days before the world championship all routine mental sessions ended, as both the athlete and the coach were busy with preparing their equipment and felt that one or two telephone conversations would suffice. BB was 60 km away from the competition site it was decided that BB would arrived at 7:00 AM before warm-up on the competition day. Unexpectedly, on the evening before the competition, BB was notified that the coach was looking for him and sounded worried. It turned out that the athlete did not want to sleep or to speak to anyone, and was nervous; in short, everything was bad. What should be done? BB felt there was a need for a first-hand examination of the situation and suggested that he get there right away. Forty minutes later BB was in the athlete's room and personally observed the situation. Indeed, the athlete was not communicative, was fatigued, and everything looked really bad. BB realized that not doing anything would be even worse, and proposed to go out for a short walk outside in the pleasant weather, see nice people, and talk about everything but the following morning's competition. There was an urgent need for a change of atmosphere. So we went out and the athlete walked 4-5 m ahead of us, and BB walked next to the coach and talked about various movies, about the film's 'hero, etc. The athlete kept quiet, but after two or three comments about movies the athlete began to correct BB's comments and examples. Unnoticeably, the dialogue switched to a discussion about films and music from films. After about an hour and a half, the athlete asked to return to the room as he felt tired and wanted to sleep. In the morning, after the morning routine, we went to the sea and then he started the first day of competition, calm and rested. The athlete achieved 6th and 7th places in two races after the first day's competition. It was a good beginning for a first day. He finished this competition with a bronze medal.

Case 3 – Judo. A year before the Olympic Games a judoka who had recovered from an accident and had undergone corrective medical treatment requested BB's help, saying: "I want to be in the Olympic Games". BB had already worked with the judoka for two years. It was already October. "What do you think, do have I any chance?" They discussed several options and decided that his options were limited, and that they had to act immediately, without wasting any time. BB devised the following plan: Begin with a recovery step, in December commence with easy judo exercises, in January do training work on Judo matches, and prepare for the March tournament with potential to earn points toward his Olympic criteria. BB was ready to provide psychological support immediately, suggested that they start the following day, and continue meeting three times per week with laboratory training such as relaxation, imagery, reaction training programs, and concentration. We discussed this program with the coach and the medical staff (e.g., physiotherapists), and they agreed to help. We began a period of intensive work including physiotherapy procedures and mental sessions, after one month, the fitness coach began training the judoka, and in December, his personal coach provided easy judo exercises.

In the end, the judoka achieved the Olympic criteria and participated in the Olympic Games. The importance of this example is that the judoka initially requested help from a sports psychologist, and the consultant (BB) strengthened his motivation and acted to immediately begin an accelerated recovery period using psychological training.

These cases illustrate that in addition to providing mental sessions to the athletes, the sport psychology consultant is expected to influence real-life situations, behavior patterns, and mood fluctuations.

Cooperation with Professional and Medical Staff

The coach plays an important role in the career of an athlete. It has been assumed that a good coach is also a good psychologist (e.g., Martens, 2004). However, in general most coaches are well versed in the physical and technical aspects of sports but lack the skills to psychologically prepare their athletes. Sometimes coaches do not always like or want any cooperation with sport psychology consultants (Blumenstein, 2001; Weinberg & Gould, 1999).

We usually begin a psychological intervention with meetings with the team officials and the medical staff, which includes a presentation of the PST program for coaches. The objective of these meetings is to describe the current state of PST in different countries (including local level), and to present our PST program for a given sport type or team. The objective of the meeting with the coaches is to provide details about the possibilities of PST, including examples of best international experiences, and to express the suitability of our PST program to their sport, team, and athletes. It is important to also listen to the coaches' requests, questions, etc. We consider these meetings successful if the coaches understood that our goal is to work together with them, and that PST, just like physical skills training, is important and that it requires repetitions, has stages, and can be measured. Indeed, it is not unusual that following the first meeting the coach will already request psychological intervention for their athletes.

It is important to establish support and understanding for the PST at all levels of the organization (officials, medical staff, coaches, athletes). We always work closely and individually with the coach, including visits to the athlete training sites and we meet with the medical and scientific staff as well, which provides important emotional support and often exerts positive (or negative) influence on both athletes and coaches.

We usually begin our new PST project by acquiring current knowledge about the specific sport event (if this is the first experience with this sport), and then we meet with the coach and attempt to understand any problems, talk with the athlete, observe training/competition, and provide a diagnosis under a laboratory setting. Only then are we ready to propose a PST plan and begin the mental sessions, visiting the athlete during a training practice or competition, as illustrated in Figure 4.1. It should be noted that the PST plan represents an extension of the 5-step PST (also see Table 3.2).

Figure 4.1. Development of PST program

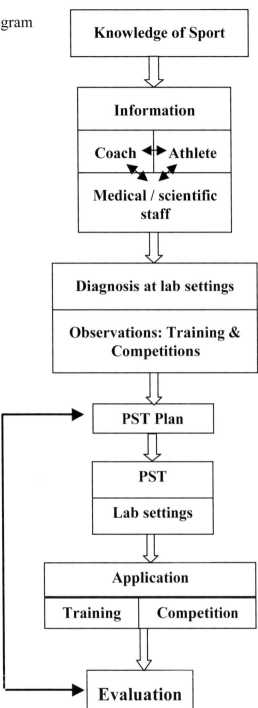

In addition to discussing the athlete's performance in the laboratory, it is strongly advised to observe athletic performance in real-life situations, such visits to practices one or two time a week (stadium, gymnastic hall. swimming pool, sea). A key element to a successful PST is to establish good interaction with coaches in training conditions, and to exchange information with the coach on the status of the athlete, including details of any difficulties he or she is experiencing. We continue with discussing future ways for performance enhancement; we sense that coaches approve of and appreciate our interest in the training process. Often these meetings provide a good setting for the generation of new ideas. Sometimes clever decisions are made, and we can get a good idea of the coach's perspective on how to deal with specific situations. We invite the coach to the psychological laboratory so he or she can now have a better understanding of our methods and the importance of our work. In addition, we often invite coaches to take part in several psychological sessions, especially during the preparation phases for competition. For example, in combat sports during a mental session with imagery of the match with potential opponents, the coach provided different tactical suggestions to the athletes on the best exercise for a given maneuver in judo, fencing and taekwondo, or different reminders about the best technique/performance to be used during competition (canoe/kayak or rhythmic gymnastics). In this way, the coach becomes an integral part of the psychological preparation and our cooperative work becomes part of the general training process.

We discuss athletic preparation once a month during meetings with the athlete's entire medical and professional staff, which includes the physician, physiologist, physiotherapist, psychologist, and nutritionist. While daily exchange of information are provided as necessary, we also hold two meeting per a year with the coach and the sport organization officials to discuss their athletes. Before an important competition, we repeatedly emphasize that we share the same common goals, and thus should have a clear understanding of their decisions.

PST training varies to suit the particular preparation phase. For example, after the transition phase, during general preparation when the coach and athlete begin the long training period, we provide various motivation talks and goal setting information during or after the training session. During that year or period, after training, we provide relaxation sessions with music (15-20 min), especially toward the weekend. Athletes undergo regular psychological sessions 1-2 times per week in the laboratory. During the specific preparation, we placed special attention on imagery and relaxation techniques in order to improve the athlete's specific technique, and give attention to self-talk techniques and self-regulation skills. BFB training and relaxation are also used intensively.

In the competition phases, a mix of all the techniques are applied, as well as specific programs such as RTP for combat sport, and special psychological training program (SPTP) for gymnastics, canoe/kayak, basketball, etc.

There have been numerous instances when the coaches did not want to commit to long-term cooperation with the sport psychology consultant, explaining "…I just don't have the time for mental training, give me 1-2 psychological techniques and I'll provide these techniques when my athletes need them or when I have time..." This was common to coaches who had several athletes, and had the privilege to select the best one for a given event, those with " …a strong character and willpower" (as coaches used to say), and were not afraid to lose one or two weaker ones (Blumenstein, 2001).

In these instances, we invited the coach to the laboratory for a demonstration, during which we explained several psychological techniques such as relaxation, concentration, imagery, and biofeedback training, and illustrated several physiological responses to the application of these techniques. These included heart rate (HR), muscle tension (EMG), and galvanic skin response (GSR), and based on these responses we could discuss the application of these techniques to achieve an optimal competition state. Often, following such meetings, the coach proposed that we "try these techniques on two or three athletes" and assigned those athletes to psychological consultations. However, there have been several cases where the athletes/coaches did not continue the consultation. For example, several psychological skills trainings for coaches were provided before the 2004 and 2008 Olympic Games, but after 2-3 meetings we stopped our activity for logistic reasons; nevertheless, we continued trying to assist whenever possible.

Cooperation with scientific staff occurred during the various seasonal physiological tests, which were given by the supporting medical and scientific staff. Following the transition phase, elite athletes underwent thorough tests measurement aerobic (cardio-vascular) fitness (e.g., VO_2max and endurance), muscle force and endurance (e.g., the Wingate Test, isokinetic tests, reaction time, and complete medical tests, such as dental, orthopedic, cardiac, eyes, etc.).

We encouraged the athletes to undergo these series of tests, and often helped by raising the level of motivation during tests, which require full athlete cooperation (e.g., VO_2max). Establishment of good personal and professional relationships with the scientific and medical staff is a crucial factor in the optimization of the training process. During a typical training season athletes undergo three sets of tests; these include thorough medical and nutritional tests, functional assessment before major events, and periodic tests per the coach's request.

Unfortunately, some coaches did not appreciate the importance of understanding (analyzing) the results of the various tests; therefore, they did not incorporate this information into the training process. It is the duty of the sport psychology consultant to convey the importance of using cutting-edge scientific and medical information in the training process.

Ethical Considerations

Naturally, any sport psychology consultant working with athletes and coaches must be sensitive to ethical concerns (see Gordin & Balague, 2005). Most of the information regarding the coach and athlete itself should be kept under strict confidence, whether a sport psychology consultant meets with team members individually (soccer, basketball) or as a group; it is not always clear what information is to be shared or withheld from one's relatives. On the other hand, part of the information may be presented to the coach in a very tactful manner so that it can be used for improving the training process.

This process is not simple and depends on the coach and sport psychology consultant's experience and ability. However, the sport psychologist consultant must always be aware of the ethical code and the principles that have been developed by professionals (e.g., American Psychological Association, APA; 1992, 2002): beneficence and non-malfeasance, fidelity and responsibility, integrity, justice, and respect for people's rights and dignity. The Association for the Advancement of Applied Sport Psychology (AAASP) adopted these ethical principles (Meyers, 1995), and later the National Institutes of Health (NIH, 2002) presented three fundamental ethical principles which guide the ethical conduct in research. These principals have implications for sport psychologists when working with athletes of all ages and skill levels: a) respect for persons, b) beneficence, and c) justice.

In modern sport there is a need for a great amount of capital to win medals, get results, and be victorious. However, sport psychologists are expected to view the athletes and coaches as people and not just as medal winners, and not to consider only the media, the publicity, and the financial aspects of the psychological training process.

A final note: Since we are mainly working with young individuals, in addition to understanding sport we should also be very sensitive to the generation gap, which brings with it specific cultural codes and unique language, music, films, books, and TV shows, etc. Understanding the inner world of young athletes will no doubt help establish deep and meaningful cooperation between them and the sport psychology consultant.

References

American Psychological Association (APA) (1992). Ethical principles of psychologists and code of

conduct. *The American Psychologist, 47,* 1597-1611.

American Psychological Association (APA) (2002). *Ethical principles of psychologists and code of*

conduct. The American Psychological Association

Blumenstein, B. (2001). Sport psychology practice in two cultures: Similarities and differences. In

G. Tenenbaum (Ed.), *The practice of sport psychology* (pp. 231-240). Morgantown, WV:

Fitness Information Technology.

Blumenstein, B., & Bar-Eli, M. (2001). A five-step approach for biofeedback in sport.

Sportwissenschaft, 4, 412-424.

Blumenstein, B., & Lidor, R. (2004). Psychological preparation in elite canoeing and kayaking sport

programs: Periodization and planning. *Applied Research in Coaching and Athletics Annual,*

19, 24-34.

Blumenstein, B., Lidor, R., & Tenenbaum, G. (2005). Periodization and planning of psychological

preparation in elite combat sport programs: The case of judo. *International Journal of Sport*

and Exercise Psychology, 3, 7-25.

Cox, R. (2007). *Sport psychology: Concepts and Applications* (6th ed.). New York: McGraw-Hill.

Garfield, C., & Bennett, H. (1984). *Peak performance.* Los Angeles: Tarcher.

Gordin, R. & Balague, G (2005). Ethical aspects in applied sport psychology, In D. Hackfort, J.

Duda, & R. Lidor (Eds), *Handbook of research in applied sport and exercise psychology:*

International perspectives. (pp 419-430). Morgantown, WY, Fitness Information

Technology.

Henschen, K. (2005). Mental practice – Skill oriented. In D. Hackfort, J. Duda, & R. Lidor (Eds.), *Handbook of research in applied sport and exercise psychology: International perspectives* (pp. 19-36). Morgantown, WV: Fitness Information Technology.

Martens, R. (2004). *Successful coaching* (3rd ed.). Champaign, IL: Human Kinetics.

Meyers, A. (1995). Ethical principles of AAASP. *Association for the Advancement of Applied Sport Psychology, 10,* 15.

National Institutes of Health (NIH) (2002). *Human participant protections education for research teams.* Washington, DC: US Department of Health and Human Services.

Ravizza, K. (2001). Reflections and insights from the field on performance enhancement consultation. In G. Tenenbaum (Ed.), *The practice of sport psychology* (pp. 197-216). Morgantown, WV: Fitness Information Technology.

Vealey, R. (2007). Mental skills training in sport. In G. Tenenbaum & R. Eklund (Eds.), *Handbook of sport psychology* (3rd ed., pp. 287-309). New York: Wiley.

Weinberg, R., & Gould, D. (1999). *Foundations of sport and exercise psychology* (2nd ed.). Champaign, IL: Human Kinetics.

Weinberg, R., & Williams, J. (2001). Integrating and implementing a psychological skills training program. In J. Williams (Ed.), *Applied sport psychology: Personal growth to peak performance* (4th ed., pp. 287-309). New York: Wiley.

Figure 4.1. Development of PST program

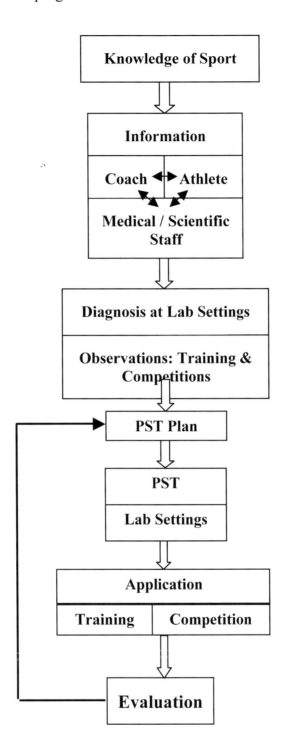

Chapter 5. Lessons and Reflections from the Field

The psychological skills training (PST) ideas presented in this book are meant to be applied to athletes and coaches. We hope that in addition to the benefits of PST to athletic performance, PST also has the potential of contributing significantly to the athlete's personal growth, which is a key factor in a successful and wholesome future.

The reader may now ask how to proceed in becoming a sport psychology consultant, and an integral part of the staff and the team. Many athletes and coaches are either somewhat naive or misinformed about what sport psychology is and what sport psychologists/consultants do. We hope that by now the reader better understands the possibilities and the practical potential for PST in the training progress. However, many young colleagues with different psychological backgrounds (e.g. clinical, cognitive, educational) who have joined the area of sport psychology frequently ask "Where does it begin?" and "What are the first steps to follow in order to achieve this goal?".

These steps include: 1) Have a thorough understanding of sport; 2) Read scientific, practical, and general literature on the particular sport type (different preparations, competitions in this sport, etc.); 3) Be able to analyze and appreciate the specific demands of the sport of choice; 4) Be ready to begin the "habit" of observing routine training practices; 5) Improve your capability of talking with athletes and coaches – try to understand what and how they operate during a single training practice; 6) Gain sound knowledge about "stars" in this sport, typing and carefully analyzing their personal qualities and professional career, and their ascent to the top. There may be potential difficulties in a particular sport (from the psychological perspective), for example in team sport – relationships among players, team cohesion, stress management, or in combat sport – problems with concentration, self-regulation, motivation, self confidence in competitive matches. The sport psychology consultant must be current with the specific psychological literature and PST on concrete sports. Finally, he or she should begin setting up routine meetings with athletes and coaches to get good ideas and comprehend their short and long term problems, and to be sensitive and sympathetic to their specific requests. We hope that by now you are ready to begin – good luck!

Evaluation of PST – What are the limitations?. One of the major challenges of PST is the evaluation of the effectiveness of a specific program/intervention. However, based on our long experience with athletes during 5-6 full Olympic cycles, perhaps one of the best indicators of the effectiveness of the PST program is if an athlete requests to continue working with the consultant and to continue the team effort, which shows that the PST is appreciated by the athlete and/or the coach..

PST effectiveness may also be assessed by following and recording the athlete's performance and achievements during the cooperation period. Elite athletes who have undergone a PST program usually notice an enhancement of their performance, with improved results and better functioning under difficult or unpredictable situations. More work is needed to establish whether this is also the case for other athletes.

We tried to be as objective as possible during BB's role as a member of the training team. Consequently, we were there for the athletes during victories as well as during defeats. Their joy is our joy, and their pain is our pain.

Following our long-term involvement with top athletes we developed an evaluation procedure, which is summarized in Table 5.1. For each of the characteristics there are three levels of evaluation – high, average and low.

Table 5.1. Procedure of PST-efficiency evaluation (for athletes and coaches) during training and competition

Characteristic	Evaluation Level		
	High	**Average**	**Low**
Continuous PST	A follows the same regime, 1-2 times per week and continues scheduled annual PST procedure	before a major competition or after a short recovery period, A returns to PST routine, 2-3 months before competition, 1-2 times per week	athletes cooperate occasionally, 1-2 times before competition or when otherwise instructed by the coach
Sport motivation level (athlete-coach report)	A completes all training tasks; copes with all exercises (specifically, swimming, running, triathlon, etc.)	complete all training tasks only if A likes this task; requires coaches' and psychologist's support during training	performs exercise and loading in full volume sporadically; in each training the athlete provides excuses for not performing or not complete the training session
Changes in training practice (attitude to training)	changes in A's philosophy* "I can", "I'm confident", "I feel good after training loads"," I like this work", etc. Positive attitude remains after mistakes	unstable behavior attitude during training	A gives excuses for not performing and when "willing" to fulfill tasks gives a capricious performance
Positive changes in athlete-coach relationship	A fully cooperates with a creative manner, mood, and humor; anticipates the next training session	unstable behavior and relationships with coach	conflicts and tension during training sessions, performance under strict discipline and fear of penalty
Performance enhancement (technical-tactical improvement)	steady improvement in technical-tactical performance; constantly correcting mistakes	unstable changes, occasional corrections of mistakes	rare, sporadic changes
PST effect (athlete evaluation – self report)	Ordinarily accompanied with verbal support ("PST helped me", "Now I can concentrate better and have more	unstable, A doesn't understand what helps, because there is no stable competitive behavior or	poor performance, difficult to accurately evaluate PST effects

	performance results		
PST effect (coach evaluation, changes in athlete's attitude to training and/or competition)	positive, stable performance changes in training and competition	unsteady changes	no significant changes in less important competitions
Confidence (athlete-coach report)	confidence", "My competitive behavior now is OK, I know what I am doing in each competition moment", etc		
Optimism (athlete-coach report)	trains with a positive attitude and with determination	unstable changes, sometimes exhibits capricious behavior ("I like this exercise, but do not like the other one")	negative, ready to quit the practice
Emotional state (athlete-coach report)			
Sport achievement	significantly stable progress in sport achievements, in major competitions (e.g., ascends from finals to medals or from 10-15th places to finals, etc)	sport achievements at an average level	lack of progress in non-significant competitions

Where A=the athlete; *accompanied with verbal or self-talking reactions

The following are notes related to Table 5.1

Continuous PST – One of the important factors in PST evaluation is the renewal of the PST routine following a competitive event or after the season's transition. BB's athletes who exhibited a high level of PST effects usually continued the cooperation for several seasons.

Athlete evaluation – A key factor, as the athlete is our main focus and we have a special interest in his/her evaluation and feeling.

Coach evaluation – An essential factor in PST effectiveness. Coaches are usually able to separate training and competition conditions in their PST evaluation.

Confidence, optimism, positive emotional state – Essential factors in an athlete's daily behavior, and the background for an effective training process.

Sport achievements – We realize that in competitive sport a successful final achievement is the ultimate goal. However, the added benefit of PST is the ability to achieve this goal with a significantly reduced stress level. Additionally, athletes may improve their mental profile, attitude to training, and personal relationships while reaching their ultimate goal.

Given our experience, we wish to emphasize again that the coach's cooperation with the psychology consultant is crucial to success in this process.

To illustrate this, we wish to share a personal note. This has to do with our experience with one of the best judokas in the country, who successfully participated in many international competitions, winning numerous medals and titles. We had good cooperation this athlete and his coach for two Olympic cycles, with excellent results (6 European, World and Olympic medals). We developed an effective psychological training program for this sport in general and particularly for this athlete, and had established a good, stable, and professional relationship with his coach. This cooperation led to multiple successes in numerous competitions. Unexpectedly, a few months before the 2008 Olympic

Games, the coach decided that psychological support was no longer needed. This decision was made against the judoka's wishes, who insisted that he wanted to continue regular psychological training, because he had faith in our work. During this crucial period the judoka was in excellent physical and psychological condition, and had also achieved excellent results in the laboratory tests typical of this preparation period (compared with previous pre-competitions tests). In numerous meetings with top sport administrators, BB made it clear that the coach is at the top of the professional pyramid and BB was merely a consultant, and that the final decisions were the full responsibility of the coach. Ultimately, it was decided that psychological support would only be provided per the specific request of the coach. In fact, BB was not allowed to intervene with the athlete preparation process until the last day before the most important event, when it was clear that the judoka was experiencing numerous problems in his fighting readiness and determination. Finally, on the morning prior to the competition, the coach requested BB's help, but it was too late. BB tried to help, and the judoka won the first match, but he lost the next match and thereafter failed in the competition. What's more, following the Olympic Games, the coach wrote in his report that the sport psychologist (who was added to the list of the "guilty" ones although he was not really a part of the final training process of the judoka's preparation) and the judoka "were not well prepared" for the competition. This example describes a rather extreme situation in which the lack of cooperation between the coach, the athlete, and the sport psychology consultant impaired the preparation process for these major events, and resulted in failure in the competition. However, there are other issues which are related to effective PST program (e.g. professional staff, officials).

The following professional team should take part in the training process: a full-time athletic trainer (if the coach is able to provide this session), a physical therapist, a team leader, a sports physician, and a representative of the federation or elite sport department. Most staff members recognize the importance of the sport psychologist and we usually interact very well. For example, the coach was constantly (1-2 times per week over the phone) scheduling BB to be present in training and competitions in order to consult with the athletes and exchange information on a daily basis. However, whenever BB initiated a consultation process, he always made a point of explaining what sport psychology and psychological skills training were. This was done without diminishing the importance of the other preparation processes and the roles of other professionals.

BB tried to clearly define sport psychology and the specific demands of consultant-coach-athlete interrelationship, including ethical norms of the professional staff and the coach and athletes. There may have been many conflict situations, such as "who is the boss?" (especially with sport officials, physicians, physical therapists, etc.), however, BB always maintained a professional position, and after 1-2 months these relationships were firmly established.

In general, the sport psychology consultant's position has to be delicately balanced among the coaches, the athletes and the medical staff. We have to be sensitive to all professions and normalize the relationships between them and our team. The worst situation is if we are a source of a conflict.

Reflections from the field:

1. PST does not replace physical training or other preparation processes. We always begin our work by talking with the athletes – What about your practice? What were your recent achievements? and so on. Following our agreement with the athlete, he/she is obligated to perform all training exercises according to a pre-set schedule founded on principles of volume, intensity, and quality, beginning from our first meeting.

2. PST can be an effective means of augmenting athletic preparation, provided that it is systematic and founded on a long-term basis (minimum 5-6 months – for initial results to be seen)

3. We are merely psychology consultants – helpers, not athletic coaches (although we are familiar with the sport), neither medical doctors nor physical therapists, and certainly not replacements for the coach.

4. A sport psychology consultant is expected to be thoroughly acquainted with the sport, to understand the difficulties, as well as the specific context of the situations in training and competition settings, and to frequently attend camps and competitions.

5. Success in the current levels of modern competitions and medal achievements in European, World championships and Olympic Games demand a world-class status from the athletes, their coaches, and the entire medical staff. Therefore, sport psychology consultants must constantly improve and upgrade their knowledge, and be aware of and apply all innovations – not only in their specific area/field but also in the theory and methodology of sport training, physiology, biomechanics, etc.

6. The sport psychology consultant intervenes in different areas, including:

   performance-related psychological skill training, conflict management and

   stress management skills, negotiation skills (with coach, athlete, medical staff, officials, etc.).

Summary and Final Remarks

   a) PST is an integral part of the general training process, where athletes systematically practice their psychological skills.

   b) PST theory and methodology should be developed for each sport type.

   c) PST is also applicable to coaches and the medical staff; there is a need for full cooperation from the coaching/medical staff.

   d) Evaluation criteria can be developed from PST.

e) High-tech equipment and methods for laboratory and training settings can be applied, with the use of telemetric feedback psychophysiological parameters, etc.

f) Ethical principles and norms are basic requirements for those who wish to be engaged in sport psychology consultant services.

g) The sport psychology consultant is expected to be fully prepared for competition stress.

h) Develop optimal positive social support for athletes and coaches.

Finally, PST requires patience; each athlete comprises a "mini" study project, which generates results that are "presented" during athletic competition.

The ideas presented in this book are intended for athletes, coaches, psychologists/consultants, medical staffs, and students who wish to utilize sport psychology as an additional tool for their work with athletes, as well as for the athletes themselves. The book provides ideas on PST programs for different sports. We attempted to describe various approaches and considerations concerning several popular psychological interventions/strategies that are applicable to different sports, and to elite athletes with different levels of psychological skills. The main idea of this book is that the PST program must be fully integrated into the training process. Within this perspective, our own approach and research findings were presented.

The sport psychology consultant feels and sees that he/she helps the athlete to achieve medals and win competitions, games, championships. He or she understands that each athlete is new research project with results, not only positive ones, and that the sport psychology consultant must be a very patient person to deal with the athletes and coaches. Elite athletes are different, and each of their cases is unique – however, we attempted to generalize our approach in this book. We believe that this book is of interest not only for specialists but also for students and young athletes, some of whom may become the next generation of applied sport psychologists.

About the Authors

Dr. Boris Blumenstein is the Director of the Department of Behavioral Sciences and Methodology at the Ribstein Center for Sport Medicine Sciences and Research, Wingate Institute, Netanya, Israel. Dr. Blumenstein received his Ph.D. in sports psychology from All Union Research Institute for Physical Education and Sport, Moscow, Russia. He was a sport psychology consultant and advisor to various Soviet national and Olympic teams, and since 1990 has served as head of psychological services in the Elite Sports Unit of the Israel Olympic Committee (including the delegations to the last four summer Olympic Games – 1996, 2000, 2004, and 2008). He is the author of over 100 refereed journal articles and book chapters, and is the senior editor of two professional books: *Brain and body in sport and exercise: Biofeedback applications in performance enhancement*, published by Wiley in 2002, and *Psychology of sport training*, published by Meyer & Meyer Sport in 2007. In addition, he is a past president of the Israeli Society of Sport Psychology and Sociology.

Dr. Yitzhak Weinstein is the Head of the Life Science Division, School of Physical Education, Ohalo Academic College, and the Exercise Physiology Laboratory, School of Nutrition, Tel_Hai Academic College, Israel. He received a Ph.D. in physiology from New Mexico State University (USA) and did a post doc at the University of California, San Diego. Between 1984 and 2003 he was head of the Exercise Physiology Laboratory at the Wingate Institute. His main areas of research are exercise physiology – metabolism, methods of recovery from exercise in elite athletes, young athletes, and physiological-psychological aspects of top performance. Dr. Weinstein's papers have been published in leading journals such as *American Journal of Physiology*, *Medicine and Science in Sports and Exercise,* and *European Journal of Applied Physiology*. Dr. Weinstein is a reviewer for several leading journals and is a section editor of the *Journal of Sport Sciences and Medicine*.